"BEDWYR, I THINK I MISSED YOUR PERFORMANCE"

BEDWYR WILLIAMS

I DON'T LIKE PERFORMANCE ON the whole. I don't go to see it. I don't know many other performance artists. I don't read about it. Hardly any of my art books (and there are not many of those) are about performance art. That is to say, I don't seek performance out. There are those that do – I can't fathom them. I don't expect anyone to come and watch me perform but if they do then I'm very grateful.

This is a collection of my performance texts that have been presented over the last fifteen years. They are written, more or less, how they were delivered at the time of the performance. They range from lists or crib sheets to complete scripts. I've left the stinkers out.

While the majority of performance is about movement and a video of my work might be more logical, I think a book is a fairer representation of the works than a mogadon[1] blow of a DVD.

The first performances had no narrative; instead I would mime or dance energetically. I thought it was good exercise for me. Nowadays, it's all talking and hardly any movement.

I used to make movements because I was scared to talk. Now I talk because I am scared to make movements.

I remember some friends coming to visit me at my lodgings and picking up a Thames and Hudson publication of *Performance Art* from my table and saying: "That's the type of bloke I really hate". It was a naked guy in a sheet and I could see their point. I want to be a performance artist but I don't want to be that man in the sheet. I've been doing it for a while but I don't think I've learnt anything specifically, or if I have, they are practical things like:

- *You don't want to perform too late or too early as you might miss the peak crowd. It's like a surfer judging a wave.*
- *If a curator puts me on first I take it as an insult. I fine them with 10% less effort.*
- *If a curator asks me to get changed in a toilet I fine them with 15% less effort.*
- *For nerves – drink beforehand but not too much. White wine is out because of acid indigestion.*
- *Choose a performance outfit that will allow you to make a quick exit (see Methodist to my Madness).*
- *There will be people in the crowd who don't like performance. You should stare at these people and break their spirit.*
- *Don't talk to the other artists who are performing beforehand (especially if they are naked).*

1 Medical: a drug used as a heavy sedative. 'A thinking man's mogadon', something that would put a man of intelligence to sleep.

- *Park your car nearby.*
- *Change out of your costume as soon as you have finished your performance and disappear for a while. No one will want to see you for a bit.*
- *Try to go outside after changing out of your costume and have a beer. It is likely that you will be joined by a silent bearded guy with a Rizla paper on his lip who says "Nice performance". Ignore him, his opinion is worth nothing.*
- *Have a wee beforehand.*
- *If someone tries to critique your performance afterwards you should make an example of them, preferably with a nasty cutting retort... Shut them down.*
- *When a performance doesn't go down well expect to have a nasty impotent feeling the next day.*
- *When a performance does go down well expect to have a nasty impotent feeling the next day.*
- *When people ask you a question along the lines of: "Are you happy with how it went?" or "How do you think it went?" It generally means it was terrible.*
- *Build up your mental and physical stamina by doing a tour of duty with Grizedale Arts.*

I can't stop it though it's a bit like being a glue sniffer; it feels like hell and everyone looks down at you but there is something that still makes you keep going.

BOX CLEVER

DE FABRIEK, EINDHOVEN, 1998

THIS WAS DURING A time when I did not speak in my performances. I also had no I.T. skills so I was living life with my ankles as well as my arms tied behind my back working as a porter. The performance was called *Box Clever* because that's what I was told to do as a 51 weeker whose security pass wouldn't even allow me into the civil service club.

I was also delivering boxes all day.

I performed a few more times over the following five years, including at an exhibition called *Sociable Realism* curated by Paul Noble, where a woman told me afterwards that I made her feel physically sick. I also performed in a show called *Virgin Oil* on Brick Lane. I didn't really now what I was doing.

In Rotterdam I gave a sitting down performance in a leather chair. An Afghan hound joined me midway and I stroked his head. Later as we all drank beer outside he strayed there was a commotion as he wandered into the path of a young Turkish guy on a moped. When he demanded to know where the dog came from a voice from the back shouted "Enschede!"

CYNGOR
Sir Ddinbych
Denbighshire

ART COCKPIT

CYWAITH CYMRU

NATIONAL EISTEDDFOD, DENBIGH, 2001

WELSH POETS HOLD THESE kind of traditional poetry slams. The competition is known as 'Talwrn y Beirdd' – Bards' Cockpit. An arts commissioning body, that is no longer with us asked me to hold an 'artists' cockpit. I was the referee while artists stuck their heads through the holes in the pit to vocalise their opinions. Below the sand, speakers clucked the names of Welsh artists in chicken speak.

CHEF

VARIOUS VENUES, 1999–2001

I DON'T HAVE MUCH documentation of this performance character. I based him on a horrible man I came across in a large industrial kitchen. He had a Bill Hayley kiss-curl that he would paste up onto his paper hat, like a horrible question mark that was made of gel and hair.

I can't remember if I spoke in this performance or not.

Chef's clothes are great because they are unique like a bishop's robes or a policeman's uniform but they have none of the baggage or significance. This performance was during a time before celebrity chefs existed.

There's a beautiful nonsense about getting people to cook for you in Andy Pandy outfits and while they are cooking for you are shouting at each other.

Get back in the kitchen, dickheads.

These images are from W139, a gallery in Amsterdam where I made a video for a show called *Game Set Match*. I got the impression the gallery hated it.

This was a hot night in Brixton. I seem to remember there was an argument before people arrived.

A woman mistook me for a skinhead in the newsagents next door to the gallery.

I went up on the roof of my friend's apartment on Electric Avenue and while I was posing for these grainy shots, I could see there was a man wearing underpants and vest watching TV in the apartment across the road. He saw me and carried on eating.

GRIM REAPER
VIOLENCE PERFORMANCE

ANGLO PONCE, THE TRADE APARTMENT, 2003

A SCHOOL FRIEND WHO WAS INTO FANTASY ROLE PLAY, SHOWED ME HOW TO AGE PAPER. HE WOULD SOMETIMES AGE SINGLE PAGES OF HIS EXERCISE BOOK AND DRAW TROMPE L'ŒIL GLASSES AT THE CORNER OF THE PAGE.

This chap appears in more of my performances. I have seriously considered the idea that he placed a curse on me when I was eighteen.

"LOOK AWAY WHILE I WELD", INSTEAD I MISHEARD "LOOK, WHILE I WELD."

This refers to a telling off I got from an artist. Artists that weld tend to bask in the macho nonsense that goes with it, talking to you with the mask in a prone position, pretending to be real welders. Dicks!

MY LONDON DENTIST CHATTING TO HIS NEW ASSISTANT OVER MY ENORMOUS MOUTH ABOUT HOW SHE USED TO POLISH COWBOY'S BOOTS IN A CASINO OR SOMEWHERE.

This dental practise, which was located on the Whitechapel Road was so small my feet stuck out into the waiting room. I once kicked a Sikh guy in the balls when the dentist hit a painful tooth with his probe.

TOOTH REMOVED IN HOSPITAL AND A RACIST MAN WITH A CONSTANTLY BLEEDING NOSE, WHO COMPLAINED ABOUT THE BREATH OF THE ASIAN DOCTOR. APPARENTLY HE ONLY NEEDED TO BREATHE ON A POTATO AND IT WOULD BECOME CURRY FLAVOURED. HE LATER KICKED THE TV CONSOLE AWAY FROM THE BED AND IT HIT HIS WIFE'S HEAD,

I have met some jerks over the years but I'd never met an old jerk. I thought it wore off in their fifties. Oh no! This guy was a bona fide O.A.P. prick.

HEAVY MET TELLING HIS GIRLFRIEND TO 'ROCK OFF'.

You don't see rockers like this as much any more; the ones in the 'pre-Internet era' who struggled to get the look right.

COUPLE THROWING DOG FOOD TINS AT EACH OTHER AND MISSING AND HITTING MY MOTHER ON THE ANKLE

This was not the same couple but I do like to imagine them also saying 'Rock Off ' to one another.

AND AS I KEEP TELLING YOU "DARLING, I LOVE YOU."

I don't remember saying this and I don't know what it refers to.

IT WAS AN *XBOX* THAT CAME THROUGH THE WINDOW, NOT A *PLAYSTATION*

I found one of my neighbours repairing a window in his house. I asked what had happened and he replied with the above.

FLICKING 4WD VEHICLES INTO THE SEA IN THE FLINT AREA

On bank holidays North Wales is over run by people in 4wd vehicles. The people that drive these are the sort of people that would commandeer the water bowsers and guard them with rifles if society were to break down in this country.

Italian restaurant in Soho when a friends meal went sour

I was eating out with some Swedish friends, when a drunk man who had been asleep when we arrived woke up and punched his friend's wife square in the face. He was taken out and soundly beaten by his friends. The window (which had a big picture of a bottle of Chianti painted on it) shook as they struck him.

Leave him alone hassle during tonsillectomy

Years ago, while I was in a hospital, I intervened in an episode of ward bullying and ended up making things worse.

Mouthy bloke angers people in a wake in another part of pub.

Here I described a man in a wake who was itching to fight. He was goading the other guests at the hotel who were not in the funeral party. This mourner was a moron.

Burnt bits of zip after the goalkeeper left his tracksuit behind the week before

I don't want to talk about this.

Thousands of hot ball bearings dropped on man

Imagine this.

Sainsburys car park "what's the matter with you mate?"

Try as I might I don't like Cockneys or their attitude: "Be Lucky!"

Reading festival naked, South Walian going ape and getting beaten up

When my panic attacks were at their worst, I went to a music festival with my brother. On the last night, we cowered in our tent as a naked South Walian, who had been screaming and smashing people's wing mirrors, got beaten up. We were worried that the lads would stumble over our tent and realise that we were also Welsh and set upon us too.

Fat kid getting the finger across the avenue

Children are horrible to each other and there's nothing we can do about it. The bully in question here was a nasty epoxy of bile and resentment.

Man trying to kick a speeding car in Liverpool – tossed in the air

This man was drunk. His barely fitting slip-ons with no grips made him an easy skittle to tumble.

The Grim Reaper with Colin Lowe at the ICA. We didn't go down well someone threw a wet sport sock that hit me on the chest.

Running over a seagull, opening it up as if it were book

Animals are often nice on the outside but nasty on the inside when they are squashed. Seagulls are nasty cakes with nasty fillings.

Sewing machine selling lad with open seams

Imagine a man with a cube of flushed flesh for a face selling sewing machines with the seams of his jeans opened, ironically at the seams, so they draped over his chunky shoes.

Middle age woman using the word "class" to describe how *Freddie Got Fingered* made me realise I was getting older

People using phrases and words from outside of their generation confuses me. On the TV recently, a woman in her fifties said she was about to get 'down and dirty' with her next guest. What on earth did she mean?

Offered petrol in the hairdresser

I don't want to talk about this.

Man offering up a wind spoiler to a car

Or this.

Monster truck crashing into the audience. A man saved a child but was killed himself. Lester Gillingham

My heart aches x2 when I see families that have lost loved ones in accidents at funfairs or while they are being entertained, like in this instance at a monster truck event.

Man's head trapped in a door of pub

On New Years Eve in Ruthin, years ago, I was involved in a crush to leave a pub. A man's head was squashed against the door frame. I couldn't see his face but I could hear him shouting.

Horse martial arts

The contrast between a horses width and it's depth is the thing that makes me wary of them.

Horses narrow from the front but long

My neighbour's underpants blue and fading

The shambles of the costume is revealed from the rear.

THE DINGHY KING

ROMANTIC DETACHMENT, GRIZEDALE ARTS, CUMBRIA / PS1 NEW YORK, 2004

I am the Dinghy King.

I grew up in other people's holidays. In the backgrounds of a thousand holiday snaps.

Costa Geriatrica as the area is sometimes called, is the strip of holiday resorts along the coast of North Wales.

A tall boy with an enormo-head and thin legs.

One day the cameras stopped clicking and the Scousers stopped Scousing.

I vowed to my people that I would bring tourism back to the bay.

There was a Jiminy Cricket type character whispering "Don't do it", into my ear. I brushed him off and broke his back with my heel.

I first saw dinghies in the garden next-door still with sand in the grooves.

As I got older, I ventured down to the promenade, I saw dinghies hanging in clusters outside fancy goods shops; hot and brand new in the sun. Inflated to pressures way beyond the lungs of normal children or kids. They lolled around in the breeze like bloated hides.

Some people came to the bay with their own dinghies; other people came to the bay and bought new dinghies. No dinghies for me.
At one end of the bay, a choc minty Shangri-la of senility – a bony island, maybe. Pensioners like drab crabs sidestep each other. Drop out opticians and drifter dentist's are bopped by the hanging dinghies as they pass.
Around the corner there is a puppet theatre called Harlequin that my brother went to once. I never got the chance. I found their pictures on a microfiche in the library opening the theatre in the Sixties with puppets dangling and dated digital watches. The theatre isn't as busy today. When it does shut down, I'm not sure how you would re-develop a puppet theatre, what with the tiny dressing rooms and what have you.

The curved grass embankment nearby with council workers, who themselves are like municipal puppeteers swinging lawn mowers on long ropes like lethal pendulums to crop the hard to reach slopes.
To the east, a Tudor style hotel is not doing so well these days. There was an occasion when the owner's son was being dropped off at a concert and his foot was flattened by the rear wheel of his Dad's car. His friends queuing outside the venue laughed at first, but then started screaming when they caught sight of his pulverised foot bursting out from the ripped seams of his fancy shoes.
I saw broken foot-pumps. I saw soggy forgotten socks. I saw men with their wet suits rolled down to the waist like overweight futuristic satyrs barking orders at their kids in kidsize wet suits in between their Cola burps.
I saw a railway carriage converted into a restaurant that had Jazz nights. The menus had pictures of a Saxophonist sitting on a crescent moon, leg dangling. I went there with an Ex and watched a bloody bad band. On the way out I saw a mound of dog turd under a bistrotheque table with a torn beer mat stuck in it, like a horrible wafer. The dog, who I took to be the culprit, was by the door with his owner, not bothered.
I saw black and white photos of men dressed like French clowns – big men.
I saw a punk bands name sprayed on a wall slowly disappearing year by year, by being coated with seagull droppings.

The band was called 4Q.

Sand doesn't get carried into town on people's shoes these days. I see the barbershop where an old man couldn't pay for his crew cut.
I can see the barber's armpits and the microclods of deodorant hanging in the hairs. I can see the barber's zero sympathy face, I can see the off duty squaddie detaching the speakers on his stereo to show me. Shifting the hair cuttings out of the way with tiny feet.
I can smell food. I can see a cool box full of blood.
The hotel where a naïve French exchange student with oval spectacles took a beating.

My parents used to take international exchange students in. One guy from Lyon gave me dead legs.

I see some lack lustre Mods and less lustre Rockers terrifying nobody; they seem scared of the locals.

It was mostly mods, but not like mods in magazines, they seemed depressed.

Rainbow Bridge; where I jogged with an ex-military man and he explained his cramps to me. He was coaching me for a mini marathon and after a few outings he said 'I think we might have a winner on our hands.' He didn't have a winner on his hands. After the race I went to show him my souvenir race T-shirt and mug. He seemed disinterested. Months later, I found a book of matches with the playboy motif outside his house. My father said that he must have got them when he was on manoeuvres.

I WENT TO THE NETHERLANDS – THEY ALSO HAVE DINGHIES ON THE BANKS OF BIG RIVERS WITH NATURIST'S SPEED GAMBOLLING ABOUT.

I discovered this grotty nudist hangout whilst cycling. It looked like the least fun you could have with your clothes off.

ON A SAND DUNE, FIVE NAKED MEN FLYING A REMOTE CONTROL AEROPLANE BUZZING THE OTHER NATURISTS ON THE BEACH.

I've never understood naturists and the concessions they make to running shoes and baseball caps and watches.
This makes me think that their priority is baring genitals. It should be all or nothing.

BEHIND THEM, A FAT MOTHER SUNBATHING NAKED WITH HER CHILDREN WHO ARE SAT AROUND HER FULLY CLOTHED AND BORED SHITLESS.

SOME HAVE BEACHWEAR. OTHERS IMPROVISE: HOISTING THEIR UNDERPANTS UP BUTT-CRACKS TO FASHION PUG THONGS.

FRECKLE FACE NOSE AND HIS HORRIBLE SISTER. LANKERS, OSMOROID, DAVID, DAVE, DAY, DAY.

A PAIR OF TWINS: THEIR HEADS LIKE LARGE BUNGS AND THEIR HOWLING VOICES AND A WORRIED MUM.

BACK IN THE BAY, ALL IS QUIET APART FROM THE SOUND OF AMBITIOUS SEVENTEEN YEAR OLDS HAVING DRIVING LESSONS IN SMALL CARS.
I AM THE DINGHY KING.

A long lost cousin of the Dinghy King was working as a pair of binoculars on the Staten Island ferry.

LLWYFAN
CYMRU

ALBATROS

NATIONAL EISTEDDFOD OF WALES /
CAMDEN ARTS CENTRE, 2005

Os oes yna rywun isio offer cyfieuthu – does na ddim

If you want translation equipment - there is none.

Mi ddywedodd rhywun unwaith fod Golff yn esgus i ddyn gwyn wisgo atha pimp.

Someone once said that golf was an excuse for white men to dress like pimps.

1. Yn yr ysgol doeddem ni ddim yn cael cyffwrdd yn y Delyn – byth. Roedd yna lond llaw o ennod oedd yn cael ei drin. Unwaith mi gymerais bluen o'r bwrdd natur a taro ychydig o dannau gyda fo. Ges i ffrau. Roeddwn yn gwisgo shorts ar y pryd felly roedd y ffrau yn teimlo'n waeth. Dwi di clywed rhai bobol hyn Cymraeg yn dweud shorts ond yn golygu trôns.

At school we weren't allowed to touch the harp. Ever. A handful of girls were permitted to play it. Once I took a feather from the nature table and brushed it along the strings. I was told off, it felt worse as I was wearing shorts. Some older Welsh people say shorts when they mean underpants.

2. Mae'r busnes (dwy law at ei gilydd) yn mynd ar nyrfs fi efo'r Delyn. Yr eiliad yna o ddistawrwydd cyn i'r dynion dwylo mawr ddechrau clapio

The way a harpist mutes the strings and then the silence and then the large hand clapping of men, annoys me.

3. Mae'n fy mhoeni weithiau fod penderfyniadau sy'n effeithio fy mywyd i yn uniongyrchol yn cael ei gwneud ar y cwrs golff neu wrth lwytho telyn i fewn i gefn Car.

It worries me that decisions that affect my life directly are either made on the golf course or whilst loading a harp into a car.

4. Ma telyn angen car mwy nag arfer iw gludo neith hatchback ddim y tro. Mae cael telyn yn y teulu yn 'lifestyle decision'. Fel cael cath sydd angen i gribo bob dydd neu rhyw bysgod trofannol sy'n mynd yn sal byth a beunydd.

A harp needs a larger than average car to transport it. Having a harp in the family is a lifestyle decision like getting a long haired cat that needs regular combing or tropical fish that get ill all the time.

Mae set o glybiau golff yn edrych yn dda mewn cefn car mawr, yn enwedig efo'r tywel gwyrion yna yn hongian allan atha rhyw cravatte. Gyda unrhyw hobi drud. Mae'r adeg llwytho offer i fewn i'r car yn gyfle da i ddangos eich hun i'r byd a'i wraig. Mae'r deifwyr yn y chwarel yn Llanberis yn gwneud hyn.

A set of golf clubs look good in the back of a big car with the stupid towel hanging out of the bag like a cravat. The time spent loading your equipment into the car is a good opportunity to show off to others. The divers in Llanberis do this.

5. Ers i mi basio fy mhrawf gyrru ryw 12 mlynedd yn ol rwyf wedi trio codi ofn ar chwareuwyr golff yn ardal Llandudno wrth iddynt groesi'r ffordd. Mae na arwyddion i hysbysu gyrrwyr fod yna olffwyr yn croesi – fel 'tasen nhw yn anifeiliaid, neu blant neu henoed hyd yn oed sydd heb arfer gyda'r ffordd fawr. Mae'r arwydd yn codi awydd arnaf iw trawo gyda fy nghar estet.

Since I passed my test some twelve years ago I have tried to intimidate golfers crossing the road in Llandudno. There are signs warning you that they are crossing as if they were animals, children or the elderly. This sign makes me want to drive into them.

6. Yn yr ysgol roedd na blentyn yn chwarae golff yn ei amser hamdden. Pan oedd yr athrawes yn holi be oeddem wedi wneud dros y penwythnos fe atebai 'Chwarae GolFF' Roedd ei 'Ph' fo yn gwneud fi isio ei ddyrnu. Roedd ganddo fo wastad tees yn ei gas pensiliau. Dwi'n meddwl fod yr athrawes wedi eu cymeryd oddi wrth o unwaith am ei fod yn beryg. O'n in chwerthin i'n hun.

There was one kid at school who played golf in his spare time. When the teacher asked him what he had been doing over the weekend he would answer "playing golff". His 'ff' made me want to thump him. He had golf tees in his pencil case. I think the teacher confiscated them once – I laughed to myself.

7. Pan o'n i'n byw yn Llundain roeddwn yn arfer chwarae pel droed ar bnawn dydd sul gyda ffrindia. Un pnawn daeth dau foi mawr efo ci a clwb golff yr un. Roeddent yn hitio'r bel at ei gilydd o un pen o'r cae i'r llall dros ein pennau. Roedd rhaid i ni roi gorau i'r gem

When I lived in London I used to play football on a Sunday afternoon with friends. One afternoon two large men with a dog and a golf club each came along and started hitting a golf ball from one end of the park to the other over our heads. We had to stop our game and leave.

8. Yn yr ysgol roedd gyn i dipyn o ofn y delyn, y delyn oedd y gwrthrych mywaf yn yr adeilad er mae'n siwr os fyswn i wedi sbio yn iawn fod yna declynnau mwy yn y gegin. Mae telyn atha dyn mawr gyda traed bach. O'n i wastad ofn y bysa fo'n tiltio drosodd ac yn sgwashio un o'r gennod.

At school, I was scared of the harps. It was the largest object in the building – although there where probably bigger bits of kit in the kitchen. A harp is like a big man with small feet. I was concerned it would keel over and squash one of the girls.

9. Ma gin i draed seis 13. Unwaith mewn siop chwareuon fe welis i sgidia golff i blant. Gan fy mod i yn cael trafferth ffeindio sgidia sy'n ffitio ac yn gorfod prynnu sgidia dros y we roedd hyn yn fy nghythruddo. Dwi'n teimlo fod o'n hawl dynol i fedru prynnu esgidiau sy'n ffitio ar y stryd fawr. Mae'r busnes fod gan dodlars fwy o ddewis sgidia na fi yn fy ngwneud i mi deimlo'n isel. Roedd gwyneb y nincompoop mewn tracsiwt oedd yn y siop hefyd yn fy ngwylltio, roedd ganndo fo lovebite ur un siap a lliw a croissant ar ei wddw.

I've got size 13 feet. I once saw golf shoes for kids in a sports shop. As I find it hard to find shoes that fit me, and have to order things on the Internet. This angers me, I feel it's a human right that I should be able to find shoes that fit on the high street. This business that toddlers have more choice than I do is depressing. The face of the nincompoop in a tracksuit working in the shop angered me. He had a lovebite the same shape and colour as a croissant.

10. Ma na rywbeth amdan plentyn yn chwarae telyn yn nhrwblo fi yn yr un ffordd a phlentyn yn chwarae golff. Ma o'n rwbath i wneud hefo seis. Mae plant mewn sbectols haul oedolion yn edrych yn stupid hefyd. Hyd yn oed

YN FWY GWIRION NA HYN YDI PLANT GYDA GEL YN EU GWALLT. MAE'N SIWR GEN I FOD PLANT SY'N CHWARAE GOLFF YN GWISGO GEL A SPECTOLS HAUL.

There is something about a child playing a harp that bothers me the same as a child playing golf. It's to do with scale. Kids in adult sunglasses look daft as well. Even more stupid are the ones with gel in their hair. I'm sure that kids who play golf wear shades and put gel in their hair.

11. YN 1999 FE ANAFODD YR ACTOR JACK NICHOLSON CI SHIH TZU EI FAB SAITH OED GYDA CLWB GOLFF. ROEDD RAID I'R CI GAEL PUMPDEG SAITH O BWYTHAU YN EI ABDOMEN.

In 1999, the actor Jack Nicholson injured his son's Shih Tzu dog whilst playing golf. The dog required fifty seven stitches in it's abdomen.

12. FE GAFODD SEAN CONNERY EI DRAWO YN EI BEN OL GAN BEL GOLFF YN Y FLWYDDYN YNA HEFYD GAN ACHOSI CHWYDD. DYWEDODD UN DYN OEDD GERLLAW FOD SEAN WEDI SGRECHIAN ATHA DYNES PAN GAFODD EI DRAWO.

Sean Connery was struck in the buttocks by a golf ball in the same year causing swelling. A man nearby said that Sean screamed like a woman when he was hit.

13. EFALLAI FOD GAN Y RHAI SYDD WEDI CAEL GWERSI TELYN YN IFANC CLUTCH CONTROL DA OHERWYDD EU BOD WEDI ARFER GYDA'R PEDALAU

Maybe kids who can play the harp have good clutch control because they are used to pedals.

14. MA NA DDYN DIREUDUS YN AMERICA YN RHOI BAW CI MEWN TYLLAU GOLFF A DYN ARALL SY'N TAFLU FYNY I FEWN I DYLLAU GOLFF

There is a mischievous man in America who placed dog dirt in golf holes. There's another who poured vomit into them.

15. GOLFF I'R DEILLION YN AMERICA
'YOU DON'T HAVE TO SEE IT TO TEE IT'

Golf for the Blind in America:
'You don't have to see it to tee it.'

16. YN 2002, YN YR UNOL DALIAETHAU FE GAFODD GOLFFIWR I FFEINDIO YN EUOG AM LADD DYN ANABL OEDD YN MYND O GWMPAS Y CWRS YN HEL PELI COLL.

In 2002, in the USA a golfer was found guilty of killing a disabled man who was going around the course picking up lost balls.

17. FATTY GOLF – YN YALE YN U.D.A. MAE'NT YN CAEL CYSTADLEUAETH O'R ENW FATTY GOLF LLE MAE'R CYSTADLEUWYR YN GORFOD PWYSA 250 PWYS NEU FWY. DWN I'M OS OES NA GYSTADLEUAETH I FATTIES SY'N CHWARAE'R DELYN

Fatty Golf - In Yale in the U.S.A. they have a competition called Fatty Golf where the contestants have to weigh over 250 pounds. I'm unaware of similar contest for harpists.

18. YN PULLMAN YN U.D.A. FE GAFODD DYNES EI ACHUB GAN DELYN PAN DDECHREUODD EI CHAR ROLIO YN OL DROSTI. FE AETH Y DELYN YN SOWND YN YR OLWYN

In Pullman, U.S.A a woman was rescued by a harp when her car started to roll over her. The harp got stuck under the wheel.

19. YN 2004, FE AETH DYNES A PENSAER CWRS GOLFF I'R LLYS AM IDDO ROI Y SAFLE BARBECIW MEWN LLE PERYG YN Y CWRS GOLFF. CAFODD EI HITIO YN EI PHEN GAN BÊL

TRA'N ISTA MEWN CART GOLFF, DYWEDODD EI CHWAER IDDI DDISGYN OHONO FEL DOLI CLWT.

In 2004, a woman took a golf course architect to court for locating the barbecue area in a dangerous place on the course. She had been struck in the head whilst sitting in a golf buggy. Her sister said that when she was struck she fell out of the buggy like a rag doll.

20. YN PUNTA GORDA YN 1969 SYRTHIODD CANOEDD O BELI GOLFF O'R AWYR HEB ESBONIAD

In Punta Gorda in 1969 hundreds of golf balls fell out of the sky unexplainably.

21. DA CHI'N GWELD FOD GYN I LOT O HANESION GOLFF MAE RHAI TELYN YN ANODDACH I FFEINDIO AR Y WE. MAE'R STORIAU I GYD AM DELYNAU YN MYND ALLAN O DIWN NEU'N CRACIO. NES I FFEINDIO UN AM GOLOMEN YN PW PW AR DELYN YN OREGON A RHYW GATH OEDD YN CANU PAN OEDD EI PHERCHENOG YN CHWARAE – DWI'N AMAU MAI CELWYDD OEDD Y STORI YNA

You will have noticed that I have a lot of golf stories, harp stories are harder to find. I've got stories of harps cracking and going out of shape. I found one account of a pigeon crapping on a harp in Oregon and a cat who sang when it's owner played the harp. I'm guessing the last story is a lie.

22. MEWN EISTEDDFOD Y CYLCH PAN YN BLENTYN ES I AR GOLL A CERDDED I FEWN I YSTAFELL DYWYLL. FE WAEDDODD RHYW DDYN GYDA CLIPFWRDD TU OL I DELYN 'WYT TI FOD YN FAMA' 'NACDW, DWI DDIM YN MEDDWL' ATEBAIS 'NA DWI DDIM YN MEDDWL CHWAITH'

In a local Eisteddfod as a child I got lost and walked into a dark room, a man with a clipboard standing behind a harp shouted 'Should you be here?' 'No, I don't think so' I replied. 'Neither do I' he said.

23. NES I WELD BAG I DDAL TELYN AR WERTH AR YR HYSBYSFWRDD YN TESCO UNWAITH ROEDD O YN Y STEIL SGWENNU BALWN GYDA DOT YR I DOT YN GALON. MERCH YN MYND I COLEG EFALLAI NEU TELYN WEDI TORRI.

I saw an advert for a harp bag on the notice board in Tesco. It was written in a bubble style with the dots of the 'i's' drawn in the shape of a heart. A girl going off to college maybe? Or from a broken harp?

24. ROEDD Y GORIAD AR GYFER TIWNIO'R DELYN YN YSGOL GYNRADD YN MYND AR GOLL O HYD.

The key for tuning the harp was always going missing.

25. ROEDD YNA DDWY DELYN YN YR YSGOL, UN MAWR AUR EFO RHYW ANGEL ARNO AC UN BACH TYWYLL. ROEDD Y GENNOD PUSHY I WELD YN DEFNYDDIO Y DELYN EURAIDD YN AMLACH NA PHEIDIO.

There were two harps at school. One big, good one with an angel on it and another smaller, darker one. The pushy girls seemed to play the big one more often than not.

26. YN AMERICA MAE YNA DELYNNAU EFO GOELUADAU YN FFLACHIO ARNYNT.

In America they have harps with lights on.

27. MAE RHAI YN DISGRIFIO TELYN FEL PIANO NOETH

People have described the harp as a naked piano.

28. NOSON TAN GWYLLT YN YR YSGOL PAN ROEDD Y RHIENI (INVOLVED) YN DOD A'U FFLACHLAMPIAU EFO NHW. FE WELIS I GIP O'R DELYN YN YR YSTAFELL FACH DRWY'R FFENEST AG O'N I'N MEDDWL FOD O BRAIDD YN SPOOKY. DAETH LLAIS OR TYWYLLWCH.

DEWCH O FANNA HOGIA, DOEDDEM NI DDIM HYD YN OED YN CAEL SBIO ARNO FO DRWY'R FFENEST

On bonfire night at school when the involved parents would bring along their own flashlamps I caught a glimpse of the harp in it's small dark room through the window. I found it a bit spooky. A voice came from the darkness 'Come away from there boys' - I wasn't even allowed to look at it in the darkness.

29. TRA'N CAEL PEINT MEWN TAFARN THEMA YM MIRMINGHAM FE SYLWAIS FOD Y DYN NESA ATA I GYDA CHWYDD AR OCHR EI WYNEB. EDRYCHAI FEL TASE YNA SHUTTLECOCK YN TRIO DIANC DRWY EI FOCH. GWRANDEWAIS AR EI SGWRS GYDA'R DYN TU ÔL I'R BAR. ROEDD O WEDI CAEL HIT Y PNAWN HWNNW GAN BEL GOLFF. ROEDD Y CLWYF AR EI WYNEB YN GWNEUD IW WRAIG DEIMLO'N SAL FELLY ROEDD O WEDI DOD ALLAN AM YCHYDIG O HEDDWCH.

Whilst having a pint in a pub in Birmingham, I noticed the man next to me had a swelling on his face. It looked like a shuttlecock was trying to escape out of his cheek. I listened to his conversation with the barman. He'd been hit that afternoon by a golf club. The wound on his face was making his wife feel sick so he'd come out for a bit of peace and quiet.

I'm at the top left of the table my chin is just in view.

This was a one off event that I really enjoyed I can see why people enjoy dressing in spooky clothes and dressing like Victorians at the weekend and sending old fashioned invites. The only thing is Monday morning when you wake up with snuff all over your face that is the time to get a fucking grip.

NEUROSIS

PERFORMANCE AS PART OF EMILY WARDILL'S FEAST AGAINST NATURE

GRIZEDALE ARTS, CUMBRIA, 2004

Emily asked me to take part in this performance. It was a long night and all the food was black.

I AM SITTING IN a tent called Trek in Cornwall. To my left, is a Dutch family in a 4x4 pickup Campervan, the father's spectacles hang around his neck by a fat foam chord. A young man beyond the hedge is making five girls laugh by talking about his skiing accidents. Adjacent, is a middle-aged man flying a kite that spins in flight making a whirring noise. When the weather is bad and I am in the tent, I can hear him outside… whirring. I have been watching the fuel gauge of my car all day, and now I'm watching the battery on my laptop, I have turned the screen brightness down and I have thirty-eight minutes left.

My name is Bedwyr Elias Williams. I'm a neurotic camper.

Neurosis became part of my life in 1994, like a tight ribbed swimming cap. My mother had a tight swimming cap, which was ribbed. In the mid eighties, when she attended swimming lessons sponsored by *Cadbury*, the chocolate company, I used to try it on. One day, it perished in the front porch on a cactus.

I was sitting in a room in Bangor when it occurred to me that I had enormous hands; not only were the fingers long but I also felt that the swirls of my fingerprints were oversized like fat laces on sneakers. This feeling lasted a week, and it was during this week that I devised a little hand mantra to stave off the neurosis. I fingered minor guitar scales or riffs over and over again using my Paisley thumb as a fret board. When anxiety levels were peaking, I would be fretting at Steve Vai speeds. Eventually, I was given beta-blockers, the scales slowed right down – like jazz. I later became a neurotic driver; my road experiences became very intense. I prayed for motorway services, counting them down as each sign passed by. The feeling of calm gained from eating was swept away as I/we edged from the motorway on to the slip road. I have developed a special butt cheek routine that is similar to my guitar fretting. There was one occasion where some Swedish girls told me about a book which referred to this feeling as 'cafard', I read the book and was the

wiser for it for about a week. One of the girls gave me some powder to ward off the 'Evil Eye', the sachet instructed me to sprinkle it out of the window. It did not seem to have any noticeable effect, except that I suffered from a bout of erectile dysfunction a month or so later. I had a handle on managing my self-medication but my self-diagnosis was a wild-goose chase. I blamed it on overindulgence, tiredness or stress. I considered, quite seriously, whether a *Dungeon & Dragons* enthusiast I'd taken lightly at school had put a curse on me. One evening, I even tried elevating myself to an even higher magical plane than the chap to try and bounce his perishing curse back at him.

I have mentioned my oversized hands and florid fingertips... towards the end of my first neuro-year. My biggish feet became a preoccupation, this, remember, was before the days of buying things on the Internet, so I had to source shoes. I would pick out shoe shops that I knew did not cater for me in order to start arguments. I would pick up baby trainers to emphasise the stupidity of the fact that toddlers have a wider choice of footwear than me.

A pair of *Converse All-Stars* I ordered once almost pushed me over the edge. The canvas basketball sneaker in a size 13.5 looked like a caricature of the shoe that I had picked from the catalogue. The rubber toecap looked more like a snapped fingernail, a screaming quick.

Happy Nightmares for Beds is a bed company in Bethnal Green. My landlord gave them a key to my flat to replace some non-fireproof divans. I had stayed home from work and almost had a heart attack when two men entered my house saying, "We've come to take a Bed away". I explained why I was so jumpy being called Bed for short but the smallest chap said, "If you're that fucking jumpy maybe you should think about leaving London, mate."

I spoil nights out for myself with little fast-moving daydreams where my bones are broken in absurd accidents falling down steps into a below pavement Tapas bar, or bending my knees the wrong way over the back of a cinema seat. These little pain trailers have Hollywood style visuals, the more I try to pin them down and nail them, the more painful and violent they become. Imagine driving your car over a pile of bones, when one of the bones pierces through the floor of your car and into the sole of your large shoe and then through your fucking foot.

UNTITLED

OVER AND OVER, AGAIN AND AGAIN

CHAPTER VISUAL ARTS / CAC VILNIUS, 2004

THE LITHUANIANS IN THIS image are listening to a children's fairytale in their own language. I'm miming to it dressed up as a fairytale peasant trapped on the roof garden in the snow. I don't know how well it was received, as I couldn't tell if it was the audio track or me that was irritating them – I suspect it was probably both. I don't like performance artists that try to bug their audience so I feel bad about this performance.

Later that night I was involved in a fracas in a bar. A sugar shaker was thrown across from the other side of the bar. It whistled passed my cheek and smashed on the wall. The police arrived and we were asked to leave. As far as I knew all I'd done was order some chicken wings. The other Welsh artists present that night still talk about it sometimes.

BARD ATTITUDE

THE MACBETH, HOXTON STREET, LONDON, 2005

My name is Bedwyr Williams. I'm from Colwyn Bay. This is Bard Attitude.

I used to start off with this line a lot but my partner said it was a bad idea so I stopped.

There used to be Bards in Wales they would pass on stories and Welsh mythologies. You do have bards these days as well, it's just that they wear black denim or black chinos.

Poets in Wales are held in high esteem and their opinions are often sought.

Before bards you had druids. What post-punk was for punk; bards were for druids.

I can't rhyme but I'll tell you some things.

I don't like this line it's clumsy.

I signed for a parcel and the delivery guy said "Thanks buddy."
I don't like that.

I struggle in *Argos* as the biros are too small for my enormous hands. My signature would often look faint. You could say that chip and pin has been a blessing for me.

They now have little pencils on the stands next to the prolapsing catalogues to test my patience.

I really hate it when one person tries to sound like a whole stadium of football fans.

At this point, I would mimic the sound of a football crowd, but in a whisper.

I saw a biker wearing a leather waistcoat over a *Barbour* waxed jacket. He gave me threatening looks while we were waiting. Later I saw him buy some aftershave and a big *Guinness* hat. I softened towards him after that.

It's hard to know with old bikers whether they are still dangerous. I err on the side of caution.

I worked with some guys as a porter in the Civil Service but I can't tell you which one because I signed the Official Secrets Act. We were given a computer, our boss said 'Something for you to piss about on, we don't want you cunts on the network.' The Head Porter was on it the most, playing card games and an oriental tile game. He used to say 'double dip' instead of 'double click'. Christmas was getting close and people were asking "What are you getting your little 'un for Christmas?". Laptop, Laptop, Laptop. One guy said 'ere, Bed, you know 'vose games on the office computer? Stick 'em on a disk an' I'll take 'em 'ome for me daughter for 'er new laptop."

One of the porters where I worked used to call me an art-freak. When he asked me to draw a picture of his girlfriend I hid a crude drawing of a penis in her hair.

The porters used to get dressed in the room. Work started at 6.30am, so I would often be tired getting in and dream-time and real-time blended together. I had a reoccurring dream at the time that the other guys had gills on their butt cheeks. One morning I was convinced that I saw gills on the guy's arse for real.

One of the guys showed me how I could get two sausages for the price of one by squashing one into the 'big rolls': "Just push the first one right in and put the second one on top and then, when you get to the till, she thinks you only got one." Then he said, "Fuck em, innit?"

The smell of the staff canteen will stay with me forever.

I was in a pub in Brixton on Saturday, and I heard some middle aged guys doing impressions of different instruments. I think they had been inspired by some wooden minstrels that were on display behind the bar. They were all bad, but one guy was really good at sounding like a clarinet. The others could see he was good but I felt that they didn't give him the praise he truly deserved.

I like Brixton a lot. I wish it had wheels and it could be driven around London like a big dangerous carnival float.

My brother had a friend called Ivor, who claimed that he never cried. He lived on a farm and had a miniature motorbike. He was like a woodland version of James Dean. I decided to put his no crying claim to the test and set a trip wire to trip him up. He cried.

Someone said that there are two types of people in the world, people who can poo in front of strangers and others who can't. I think this is very obvious. I've been in hospital a few times, my greatest fear would be to have to do a ward poo.

Now, they have modern consoles on sprung arms with a phone and a TV. Whilst waiting for a tooth extraction in hospital I saw a cantankerous old man kick his out of the way. It bounced back and hit his wife in the face. She started to cry.

Another guy who came into the ward for some nose work told me when I said that he had to be nil-by-mouth after the operation; "Fock it, I'm getting a sarnie." He was sick all over his trousers and into the plastic container that contained his sandwich.

This guy was typical of a type of coastal North Walian: Apathetic to a fault, as well as being pathetic.

I was eating a sandwich in a seaside town in North Wales when a seagull came down and stole half of my baguette. Later when I was browsing in a bookshop the other end of town I heard a Welsh learner explaining a similar story to the shop owner. When I told them of my experience, the learner seemed disinterested and left in a bit of a huff.

Welsh learners often give up on vocabulary and try to fit in by mimicking the accent.

We have a lot of Grow-Your-Own Clothes-Hedge monkeys in North Wales. We had one as a lodger. Once, he showed me how to make my own pasta. He also made a wind chime out of slate. As soon as my back was turned he was telling my girlfriend how insensitive I was. He wore yellow corduroy trousers and shoes that I think he made from a kit.

I hate Crusties.

I once ended up sleeping on the floor of a posh house in South Wales, drunk. In the middle of the night a mustachio-ed fucker in red needle cords caught me having a wee outside. He told me off quietly in a very posh English way, like a mouse holding a court martial. His house was full of shipping paraphernalia, half opened logs, barometers and silly maps. There was one ship in a bottle, I thought later, that I would have liked to force him into the bottle arse first so that his face would become the cork. In the morning, his wife who I assumed would be called Imogen would find him.

I have always had big feet and as a child I had to take part in a play at Sunday school. It was loosely based on Blind Date but with a biblical slant. I had to dress as a woman but I couldn't find ladies shoes that fitted. I had to wear pointed men's slippers instead. I heard someone say that the slippers looked shit afterwards.

A Dutch girl once told me 'If you could speak Dutch and we were not speaking English, I would tear you to shit.'

I think this girl, now woman, is a singer.

Five years ago, I went to a cheese and wine party, there was a guy there who was hoping to join the police. He kept referring to me as 'Big Man'. It was police intimidation and he hadn't even joined yet.

Worse still a couple of years ago a former school classmate slowed down in his panda car and asked me if I was behaving myself.

Small men quite often try to make me look silly in front of ladies. They give me the smallest cup or try my shoes on when I'm relaxing

Someone once told me that I don't hug people properly.

There's too much insincere hugging these days. A curator hugged me once I couldn't tell if he was being sincere but he was making a ticking sound with his mouth as came in for the embrace.

A guy who I worked with in London once said 'When you go to Amsterdam, go to The Grasshopper and tell them I sent you." He also once said 'Were you working here when I had hair down to here?'

Nougat

This is a story about how I got caught out in a Nougat selling scam in the city of London. A pretty girl convinced me to buy some nougat to raise money for Parisian orphans. She short-changed me to the tune of £17.00. I went to the Police and that evening two detectives came to my flat. I explained that the nougat was a bit dry - they concurred.

Ernie brass rubbing kit

Press-ups are bullshit / stop my own heart

Squat stew in Vienna – dog called Babylon

This was the worst meal of my life a mini-market soup of store cupboard leftovers. It was finished off with a jar of pickled onions poured in by a chef crusty. I hate Crusties.

Man in the junction of Tesco with a disposable camera. When I hooted he gave me the finger

I don't remember this story.

Flute

I sold a flute in a lay-by so that I could buy my first computer. The farmer I sold it to asked me to play scales for him in the passenger seat of his 'Piggot' which is an unusual Welsh pronunciation of Peugeot.

Folded up picture of the previous occupant's face

The previous occupant of my house had hidden a photograph of himself bungee jumping under the stairs.

Carrying Dumbbells on a train to Edinburgh was a stupid idea. I almost left them in Crewe and the weight on top of my luggage was like having a small stocky man stowed away in my luggage.

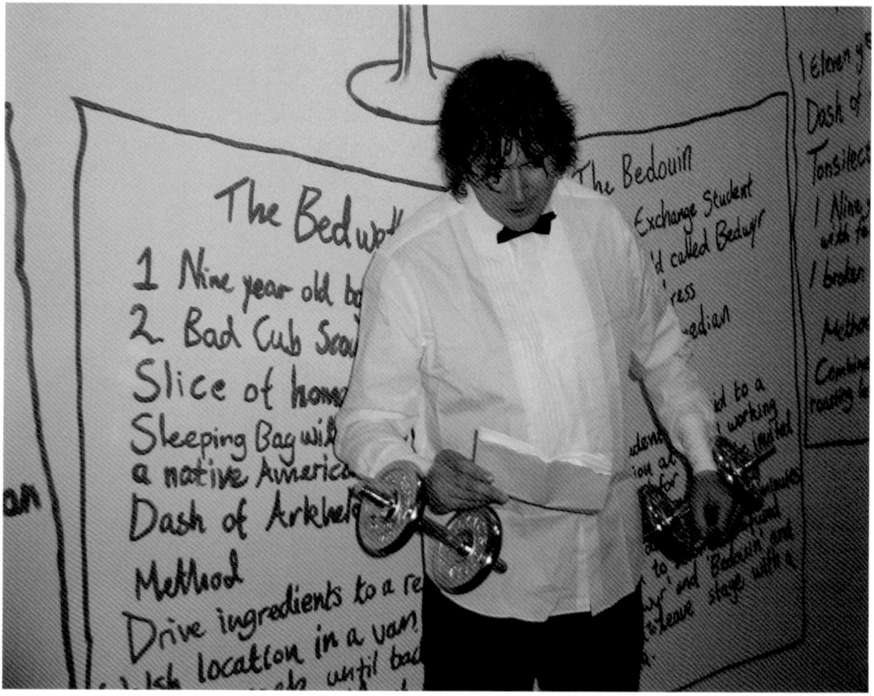

BARD SHAPE
SEAMUS HARAHAN / BEDWYR WILLIAMS
COLLECTIVE GALLERY. EDINBURGH, 2006

I was going to talk about Cambridge, but nothing happened.
I would never start a performance with a line like this anymore.

The only things that happened were that we had a Chinese waiter who looked like Ronnie Corbett and I bought some kitchen knives on the sale in Saffron Walden.
or this.

Also the American receptionist at the hotel referred to me and my girlfriend as 'Dudes'.
maybe this.

I'm in Bard Shape and I've been getting in barder shape for the last five years.

I've got Bard posture.

1. I went to see an Osteopath in very small premises about my back.
I think I got a bit emotional talking about the eighties and my hell with smaller people.
She said I should be proud of my height and that her sons were strapping lads and that they were proud of their height. Mothers always think their sons are big.
Later that week I saw her looking at yoghurt in the supermarket. She was off duty but I could see her white uniform peeping out of her jacket.
I pulled my shoulders back and decided to walk past her with good posture.
I caught her eye and smiled as I walked past, I think I freaked her out a little bit.

2. I bought some dumbbells, I said that they were for a performance, which is true but actually I wanted them to tone up. The girl who sold me the dumbbells smelt of biscuits.
Girls who work in sport shops are even ruder than the boys.

I found a regime on the Internet that required a bench. I didn't have a bench so I improvised one out of a pouffe and a storage unit/chair where I keep my newspapers.

I think I used too much paper and it broke underneath me and I really hurt my back. When I got up to try and fix it the first thing I saw was a magazine with a picture of a monkey screaming on it.
One day, the coal man saw me doing my routine and I think he was about to squeeze my muscles when I moved my arm away.

3. A guy told me in toilet in Llandudno once that if I built myself up that I would be a big bugger.

4. I found a picture of the previous occupant of my house bungee jumping. The photo had been folded really small and hidden under the stairs.

You know about this.

5. I saw a horrible kid in a tracksuit throwing chippings in the car park of a small zoo. The parrots looked like they hated them.

6. I went running on the beach a few weeks ago. I was really exhausted, and while I was recovering in the car I noticed two old people shouting in a conservatory of a bungalow. I couldn't hear what they were saying.

This motif (it's not really a motif) appears again in the performance 'Stepping Razor'
I had recently returned from Venice after a residency during the Biennale in 2005.

7. I'm dressed like the man I disliked the most while I was in Venice.
He lived with his petite girlfriend and two cats in the apartment opposite mine, I liked the cats because when the owners were out they would climb all over the kitchen tops licking plates. I once saw one of the cats fall asleep on his laptop because it was warm. If only it could have deleted some of his files as well.

I was wearing a grey tracksuit the type that cockney men and other types wear to touch and play with their bellends in public.

This man was one of those tight tendoned men who always walk on the balls of their feet. A tense, tanned twat. He used to parade around in his pants doing weights. In fact, one whole wall of his apartment was a kind of climbing exercise wall. I used to look at him through the zoom lens of my video camera plugged into the TV.
Italian TV is appalling.

Welsh TV is similar, always pairing Old Men with young 'chicks' to host things.

In between porn light, I would flick over to watch this horrible man in the flat opposite. A bit like one of my favourite films *Rear Window* by Alfred Hitchcock apart from the fact that my legs weren't broken. Although actually I could imagine him stamping on my legs to break them with his girlfriend watching.

While Signor Dickhead was working on his laptop, his girlfriend would mooch around in baggy pyjamas. The trousers of her pyjamas were way to long and they dragged along the floor, I thought that was an affectation to make herself look cute. I could imagine her stale coffee breath from across the street.

People who make a fuss about coffee and it's quality use this apparently harmless pedantism to hide or mask other major character flaws.

I couldn't figure out what he did for a living.

One morning on the rubbish bins outside he'd put a notice, he'd probably designed it on his laptop, saying "Incivili!!!!" I think that means 'Uncivilised'.

Where the trash was meant to go seemed to change from day to day. One day I was putting out my rubbish just a carrier bag of leftovers and some tangerine peel. The bin was full so I left it on top. From above came a whistle and there he was with a cat in one hand and a dumbbell in the other.

"No, no, no, no!"

I could see his face properly now, it looked like God had used calf muscles for his face as well as his legs.

"Not on there", he shouted

"Where should I put it?"

"Not there!"

"......?"

"Over the bridge, not there."

"OK, I'm sorry I didn't know."

"Well, not there, don't put it there."

"OK. I'm sorry."

"Yes well...."

That night, when I was showering in my usual squat position I wrote "Fuck you" in reverse on the window so that he would see it when he was having his muesli the next day. When I checked from the street I realised that he wouldn't have been able to see it.

I found the correct place to take my rubbish. There was a woman sunbathing there on a lilo.

I'd been in Venice about 2 weeks when I found a chrysalis inside a jar of chillies that I had bought from the supermarket. I decided to take it back. I showed the chrysalis to a woman with an enormous nose who was at the checkout. She pulled a face not unlike the keep fit git and pressed a buzzer. From behind a two-way mirror a small man who looked a lot like Nietzsche.

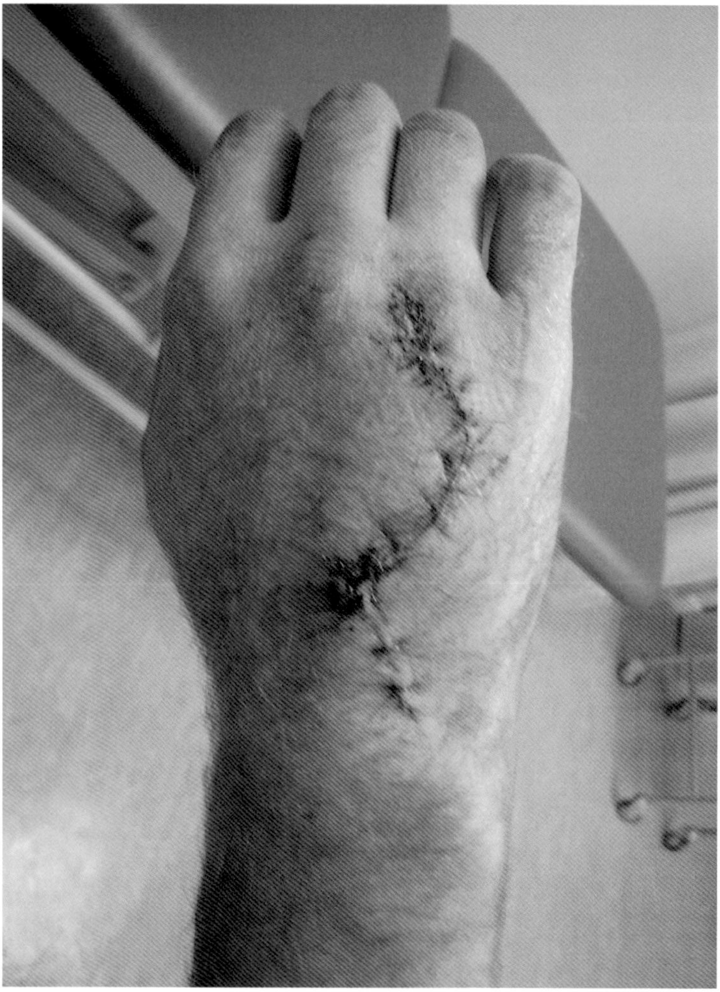

The injury to my hand means that it is unlikely I'll ever perform the cufflink / Bad Shape performance again because of the strain to the back of the hand which is a vulnerable part of the body.

He came and had a look and sniffed it and then shrugged his shoulders and returned to his office. I was given a replacement.
Every time I saw him after that he smiled I felt we'd made a connection. I imagined behind the mirror he was working on something 'hush-hush' and the mini mart was just a cover. I saw him carrying a load of miniature mattresses.

I once saw the big nosed woman on her day off on the water bus. She looked tiny but very smart, all in black. I smiled but she scowled she probably thought "It's that loser that had the chrysalis in his chillies".

When I see people that serve me at the supermarket on their day off I feel involved in their lives.

Dry skin problems.
Vittorio said that I was delicate like a little flower. I felt like I was shaving with stinging nettles everyday. I had to start moisturising. I'm sure that the big nosed lady at the supermarket smirked when I bought some *Nivea* face-cream.

People, mostly women, scowl at me all the time.

Parents stopped for speeding. Vittorio not interested so...

My parents were stopped for speeding in a water taxi. My host didn't seem interested when I told him.

COUNT POLLEN

SEVEN SAMURAI

GRIZEDALE ARTS, TOKYO, 2006

This a list of things I speculated might be worse than sneezing in public in Japan.

ATCHOO, BLESSYOU, THANK YOU, GEZOENDHEIT, EXCUSE ME

YOU ARE EATING SUSHI WITH FRIENDS AND A RAVEN SWOOPS DOWN AND STEALS YOUR NORI

YOUR CHOPSTICKS CATCH FIRE BECAUSE YOU ARE EATING TOO QUICKLY

YOU POUR GREEN TEA INTO YOUR LAPTOP IN YOUR HOTEL ROOM BECAUSE THERE'S ONLY ONE PLUG

YOU SPILL RAMEN ON YOUR NEW SHORTS

YOU DROP YOUR NEW SHORTS INTO YOUR RAMEN

YOU SIT NEXT DOOR TO A MAGNETIC MAN IN A PATCHINKO PALACE

YOU TRY TO WASH YOUR SPECTACLES IN A SPECTACLE BATH AND THAT RAVEN IS IN THERE AGAIN TAKING A BATH

YOU HAVE A PANIC ATTACK IN TOKYU HANDS

This is the best chain of shops in the world bar none.

YOU DROP TEMPURA INTO YOUR TURN-UPS AND DON'T NOTICE FOR A MONTH

This was a difficult thing to explain to my interpreter not to mention the woman signing.

YOU DROP TURNIPS INTO YOUR TURN-UPS

I'm referring to small Japanese turnips.

YOU STUB YOUR TOE ON THE WAY INTO A TEMPLE

THE HOTEL MAID SEES YOUR WHITE WIG AND YOUR FLIGHT SOCKS DRYING IN THE SHOWER AND THINKS YOU ARE CRAZY

YOU DRIBBLE ON YOUR HYPNOTISTS HAND

I had hypnotherapy to cure my fear of flying so that I could go to Japan.

YOU UPSET SOME GUYS IN A FASHION BOUTIQUE BY LAUGHING AT THEIR CRAZY SHOES

The golf trousers inflamed the skin on the performers legs, what were intended as plus fours for me served as full length trousers for her. The signer refused to wear a costume.

You get saki hiccups

You take your shoes off in a restaurant and your feet look like lizard feet

You forget your Roy Orbison voice in a Karaoke club

Someone blinds your coy carp with a lazer pen

You put too much talcum powder on your toes so your feet look like they are dead

You fall on your clear umbrella and impale yourself on it

A sticky sweet falls into your armpit while you are sleeping

Your father mixes up the words 'Tofu' and 'Futon'

Someone gets lipstick on your digital camera

Thirty bees fly into your sleeping bag and sting you

You have nightmares about a DJ made out of cheese

The translator refused to entertain the idea of a DJ made of cheese. She said Japanese people wouldn't accept it she wanted a DJ coated in cheese. I had to insist in the end.

You find a tooth in your ashtray

You see a fish with big lips waiting to die and he breaks your heart

A fish with big lips sees you and you break his heart

You try out a mini trampoline in a department store and break both your legs

Someone draws cat whiskers on your face while your asleep with a permanent pen.

Petty Crimes & Midemeanours

A Collection of Humourous and Harmless Lawbreaking

B. Williams - Grizedale Arts

CONDUCTOR FINED

Denies He Had "8.30 am Feeling"

A Liverpool Corporation bus conductor, Joseph Glover Edwards, aged 46 of 8D Paddington Gardens, Liverpool was fined £3 in the City Stipendiary Magistrates court today for not behaving in a civil and orderly manner while carrying out his duties on the morning of April 2. He pleaded not guilty.

Donald Harris Brandon, buyer, of Newstead Old Mill, Liverpool, said Edwards tried in vain to bar his son Rodney from going upstairs at Mill Lane, saying "If you thin k I am going upstairs to get the fares when we are only going to Old Swan you are mistaken.

Edwards was abusive and swore. Edwards in evidence denied stopping the boy from going upstairs. Mr Brandon spoke to him in a very abrupt manner. Mr Green (prosecuting) – Had you the 8.30 am feeling? -I don't think so.

CUE THEFT ALLEGED

After a man dashed from the side door of the British Legion Club in Westfield Street, St. Helen's, last night police found a billiard cue in nearby entry. St Helen's magistrates were told today. Andrew McCLure 52 year old unemployed machinist of 19 Atherton St, Prescot was accused of stealing the cue worth £1 7s 6d. He was remanded on bail until Monday.

STOLEN FRUIT

"Lots of other boys steal fruit. Why would my son take the rap for the loss?" a mother said at Hoylake Juvenile Court today.

Her 13-year-old son who pleaded guilty to stealing plums and pears from the garden of a house in Meols Drive, Hoylake, was granted and absolute discharge on payment of 4s costs.

BOY'S HANDIWORK

Model Rabbit Made from Stolen lead flashing. A model of a rabbit made of lead, by a 10 year old Huyton boy, was shown to the magistrates at Prescot Juvenile Court today. When the boy pleaded guilty to stealing 7lb 4oz of lead flashing from a factory roof in Ellis Ashton Street, Huyton. Chief Inspector E Sherlock commented "One may admire his handiwork but this is not quite the right way to get the materials for it".

Chief inspector Sherlock said that the manager of the factory saw that a piece of lead flashing two feet square has been removed from the roof. The boy admitted taking the lead.

The lead had been melted down in a jelly mould and the rabbit shape was still hot when the officers called at the boy's house. The boy's father told the court that his son had made the rabbit for his grandfather with the hope of getting a fishing rod for his holidays.

The boy was given an absolute discharge on payment of 15s costs.

DRIVERLESS CAR

Birkenhead Man Failed To Set Brake – Fined

Mrs Marion Robbins, of 10 Norman Street Birkenhead, was standing be her front gate when she saw a driverless car running backwards down Bidston Avenue. It crossed the junction with Park Road North and collided with a "Keep Left" sign. She telephoned the police and Constable Prescott found that the handbrake of the car was in the off position.

He later saw the driver, Frank Stead Murfin 50, of 23 Bankside Road Birkenhead, who told him he had been to a rugby match. He parked his car in Bidston Avenue and thought he had set the handbrake.

At Birkenhead Magistrates Court today Murfin, who did not appear, was fined £5 for failing to set the handbrake on April 27

SHOCKPROOF

-But not for Thief

The thief who stole ac water-proof, shock-proof watch from a jewellers display cabinet at Seacombe Ferry landing stage last night was for a shock today. He will not be able to use the watch unless he calls round to the jewellers and asks for the half-dozen vital parts of the movement which they removed before putting the watch in the case. The watch which was part of a display in a showcase owned by Williams Brothers, Hachins Hey, Liverpool. One of the partners in the firm , Mr Gerald Williams who lives at 21 Meadowside, Walassey, was passing the case on his way to Liverpool this morning when he noticed that it had been tampered with. The lock had been forced during the night and the watch removed.

"The thief wasted his time" said M Williams." Before putting the watc es into the display cabinets we alwa remove some of the movement as precaution. The thief has a usele watch on his hands. "If he cares to ca round to have the missing par replaced I should be delighted to di cuss the matter with him.

TOSS PLAYERS FINED

Two Men were fined £1 by Presc Magistrates today when they adm ted playing a game of chance name TOSS. In Manor Farm Roa Huyton.

Williams Pitt, aged 27, of 42 Ald Avenue Huyton and James Cann aged 42 of the same address admitt the offence, and were stated to ha been observed by the police playi the game on spare land at the rear a Hotel in Manor Farm Road. Wh the officer approached the game broke up but the two defendants we detained.

GIRL FINED £2

Kept Gloves She Found Outsi Ballroom

Sheila Mary Heaton, 20 years old c ton worker of 78 Hoyle Stre Warrington, who picked up a pair gloves outside a Warrington ballro was fined £2 at Warrington today f stealing by finding. She was a ordered to pay 35s restitution to t owner of the gloves, Irene Mur Wood, of 267 Lovely La Warrington.

Miss Wood told the magistrates th when she was on a bus she s Heaton wearing her gloves. Detecti Constable Brewer said that Heat told him " I didn't do anything abo them but just picked them up a wore them home I didn't tell anyon

SCOOTER CHASE

Three Boys Who Broke Greenho Caught

Three boys who ran away af throwing stones and breaking gl panes in a greenhouse, and the ow of the greenhouse, and the owner the greenhouse, Mr George Brown

VIRTUAL GRIZEDALE

THE A FOUNDATION, 2006

For this performance I gathered harmless crime stories from the Liverpool Echo. I asked a local theatre group to come and re-enact them for me. There was a misunderstanding about costumes.

THE ONLY SAFE CIGARETTE IS
A HUSBAND IS A BACHELOR WHOSE LUCK FINALLY FAILED

NEVER.
GREAT TALENTS HAVE SOME ADMIRERS BUT FEW FRIENDS
GREAT BRITAIN IS FULL OF WILLING PEOPLE SOME WILLING TO WORK OTHERS WILLING TO LET THEM
AND TALK LESS
THE BEES ARE GOING ON STRIKE NEW. THEY WANT SHORTER FLOWERS AND MORE HONEY
IT IS APRIL AND I AM BLIND
A CAREER GIRL IS ONE WHO WOULD RATHER BRING HOME THE BACON THAN FRY IT
A WELSH ELDER ANNOUNCING NEXT SUNDAY WE WILL BE HOLDING OUR ANNUAL ANNIVERSARY, SAME AS WE DO EVERY YEAR"
THE SUN WITH ALL THOSE PLANETS REVOLVING AROUND IT AND DEPENDENT UPON IT CAN STILL RIPEN MY TOMATOES AS IF IT HAD NOTHING ELSE IN THE UNIVERSE TO DO.
A PESSIMIST SEES DIFFICULTIES IN EVERY OPPORTUNITY. AN OPTIMIST SEES AN OPPORTUNITY IN EVERY DIFFICULTY
BE ALERT BRITAIN NEEDS LERTS.
THE FIRST CASUALTY IN A WAR IS THE TRUTH.
You do NOT FIND ATHEISTS IN A LIFE BOAT

THE FLORIST

AN EVENING OF OFF THE WALL PERFORMANCE

HAYWARD GALLERY, 2007

Huw Jones was a gardener who ran a florist business around the corner from where I grew up. He seemed like the last piece of a bygone era in an area that was filling up with very dull people. He made a note of all the sayings and maxims that his customer would relate to him. He would write them on the backs of card and hang them from the ceiling around his counter. He didn't censor them so there were some that maybe wouldn't go down so well these days.
At the Hayward gallery I performed a very Spartan performance reading out these quotes. I look very unhappy in the image of the performance because I was.

"Sunday is not a sponge to wipe out all the sins of the week"

"Who gives a child a home builds a palace in kingdom come"

There is a porn film of the same name.

"Television addicts usually develop a small head and a large bottom"

I'm always impressed with shy people with big rude bottoms.

"In baiting a trap with cheese always leave room for the mouse" – Some women are like fancy cakes. Colourful dressing and no substance.

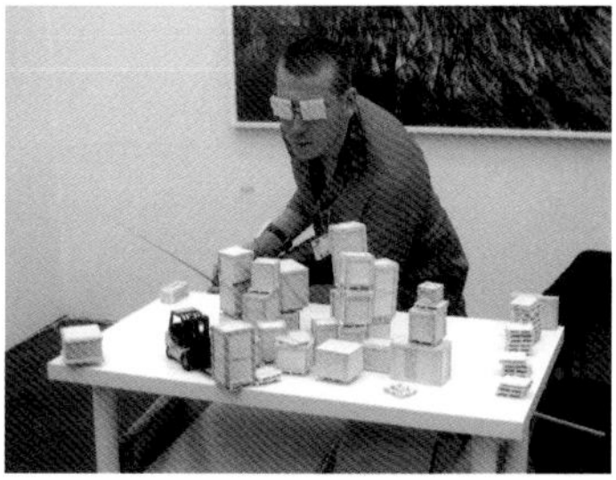

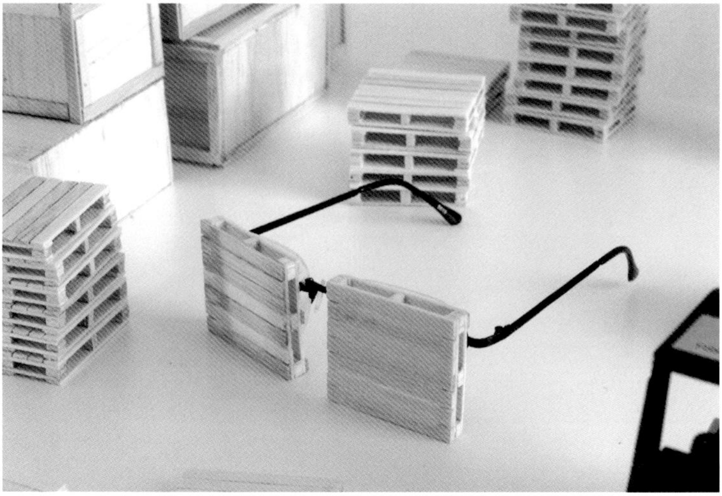

DH HELL

STORE GALLERY, 2007

This performance depicts the punishment I would like to hand down to the courier or couriers who destroyed a piece of my work in 2006. They were to be taken away and forced to stack tiny balsa pallets and crates – with a cheap radio controlled forklift. I performed this on my gallery's stand at Frieze Art Fair. I think I was putting collectors off.

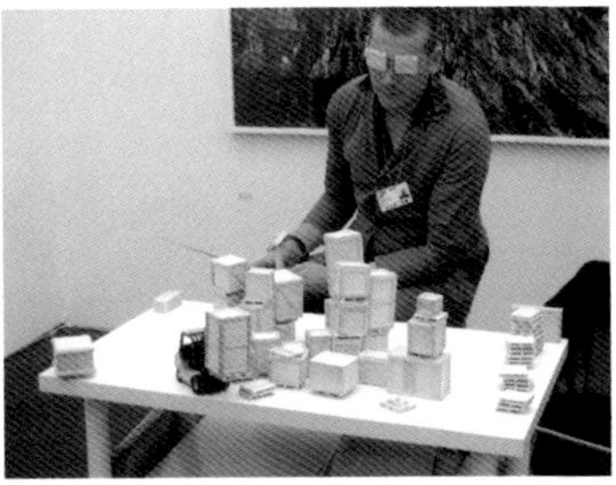

BEDWYR WILLIAMS

If you cannot sleep don't try counting sheep, try talking to the shepherd

METHODIST TO MY MADNESS

A THIN RED LINE (LIVE)

176 PROJECT SPACE, LONDON, 2008

A performance usually begins with an email – it's from someone who tells you that they like what you do. On some occasions it begins with a phone call. I once accepted an invite whilst cycling it made me feel good about myself, like a talented Frenchman being offered a promotion on holiday. They want a performance and sometimes they give you a title to work to. Where does performance begin and end?

A few years ago, I was invited to perform at a group show opening and was surprised to see that my Estate Agents were going to be exhibiting with me. I then realised it was one of those stupid artist duos who only use their surnames.

Apart from a few notable exceptions duos are people who are scared to make work on their own.

Denny & Snook. Hopkins & Bosch. Higgins & Piggins. Would I be foolish to imagine that these people seek each other out in the same way that solicitors searching for partners with quirky names do?

Nobody wants to team up with me because of my boring surname. I'm always a little envious of the safety that being in a duo provides; there is always someone to lean on. A problem shared is indeed a problem halved. But never forget that an artist's fee shared is also an artist's fee halved. That must really Rankle & Rankle.

When I perform I always choose a costume that I would feel comfortable wearing if I had to make an escape in the catastrophic event of a bomb blast or an earthquake. An outfit that I would be happy to be rescued in. Those souls who perform naked and covered in paint run the risk of being found by a fireman or a policeman or even an earthquake dog under the rubble naked and covered in paint.

Naked performance is a mug's game.

And though it may well be that the dust from the explosion sticking to the performers body might look quite good. The friend who came along to doc-

ument the performance has probably perished – crushed under the rubble or overcome by fumes. He won't have got any shots of you... that you can use! Statistically, a number of you in the audience will dislike me and what I'm doing now. Much like the man in Camden Arts Centre with a collapsed face sitting cross-legged on the floor with two drawing pins in one of his soft shoes and a single drawing pin in the other scowling at my every move. If only I could have his fingernails fall out in his sleep and then force him to pull the drawing pins out of his soles with his nib less digits.
Not forgetting the serious minded among every audience. Hating me quietly and cleverly while I put myself through my paces. I never want to show my bottom to people that may grow to dislike me.

My English teacher hit the nail on the head when she said that there's nothing worse than realising that someone doesn't like you.

It's often the case that the performer must get changed in a gallery office. I like to keep my outfit there beforehand so that my transformation is as worry free as possible. Gagging on the smell of coffee, computers and curator musk, I stow my wallet and mobile phone in my shoes for fear they will be stolen. There is no reason to think that theft cannot happen in an art gallery. I have my quick nose around the office; Post-it notes with exotic artists names and phone numbers, the elastic bands in a jar, a Polaroid of them with an artist they really clicked with and still keep in touch with. That's when the uncertainty starts and your host sticks their head around the door and asks if you're nervous and if they can get you a beer or something.

This is to make themselves better for not paying you properly or sorting out a room.

'I've got one thanks.'
I seldom have to share this changing room with another artist. Like boxers, performance artists try to destroy their 'opponents' confidence beforehand. They will do this by eating a stuffed vine leaf or a fig or any of a number of 'Fucking look at me foods', and then offer you one with oily fingers. Friendly, then aloof. London, then Nice. They mean to destroy you. They are going to go out there to scream and holler and paint their feet blue. But before they do while they get into the zone, they will prey on you for fun.

This wears me down.

Although I lie at night worrying about my performance, agonising over details, I take secret pleasure in watching artists that have problems with incompatible DVD players at the last minute. Staring into the plastic case for an answer. In Amsterdam, I saw a Swiss American artist in tears because of a broken projector. As a gesture of international support I asked, 'Can I get you a coffee or something?' She said; 'No, I can't think of such things now'.

I saw a bald man repeat that nasty mantra 'cuntcuntcuntcuntcunt' as he tried to repair a broken Theremin before a performance. A decaffeinated weekend, Brian Eno, his own kids hate him.

A Theremin is the ultimate masturbatory instrument.

So my own fears of a bad performance or a bad response terrify me. Frightening thoughts hurtle through my mind all at once before I start.

A woman in a cone hat hitting a tambourine whilst walking around in a circle with a spotlight following her on the television once when I crept downstairs.

A walking stick floating upright above an invalids bed.

A pincushion in the style of a Victorian ladies shoe made out of metal for a Victorian woman with a child size foot being used as some kind of toffee hammer to smash my bottom teeth.

The sound of teachers scraping their yoghurt pots clean in a staff room.

Walking down a bend in the stairs and coming to a door, behind the door is an old woman. Her breath like glue vapour. UHU, UHU.

Tooting Bec lido in the darkness: A ghostly swimming gala, the trunks they are wearing should tell you that they are pre-war people. Imagine being there now; corpse feet kicking your head as you drift out of your lane.

I hate swimming pools - like libraries with water. The same grey bods just wet with less clothes on.

A story someone told me of a school with a swimming pool under the assembly hall: I once dreamt of kids collapsing through the floor with their lunch and drowning with coleslaw floating around them. They would hear the shrieks of the women from the canteen.

A swimming pool at night is indeed a troubling thought.

Ages old poo poo. Ages old dog poo poo.

A duvet that ain't airy feels dead between your fingers. Like flippin flesh.

A middle-aged woman chewing treacle toffee and then when they become soft and chewy, letting them fall into your mouth one after another. She laughs through her nose as she piles more of the black slabs into her mouth.

A window cleaner his tapered ladder constantly wet like a ship's prow. An aluminium coloured *Joe Camel* with pissy steel breath staring at me through my bedroom window. Disappearing behind a curtain of grimy suds then swiping himself back into view with his squeejee before disappearing again.

Some old people stare at you when you are a kid with a face that rings out with the blue gloom of ages. It's as if they are trying to warn you with tortoise paced facial charades.

The second staircase in a house:

A friends discarded towel falls to the bathroom floor and forms a face. A flannel floor gargoyle, which you must kill before taking a shower.

This was my pulpit. A gallery couldn't afford to send it back to me so it had to be destroyed. People are reluctant to ship artworks back to Wales because of the extra cost.

To be imprisoned under a cattle grid. You hear a car and shout. As the car approaches you scream but the closer the car comes the louder the engine noise becomes masking your hoarse pathetic gaspings.

On a residency with five others in a mini bus heading back after a day out when the breaks fail on a mountain pass.

Londoners who quit the city at Christmas look forward to leaving the city and chilling out with their families and seeing old friends. Not knowing that they spoil everything for everyone else – know alls. Trying to get the most unusual presents. "I don't watch much Television etc. etc." "Too busy. Blah blah." Quietly critical of everything and everyone, like rude astronauts returning to earth.

This is a place where all the TV in the UK is made yet none of these wise-asses watch TV.

An insomniac lock keeper troubled by images of the lock full of water and then empty over and over again.

A husband and wife drug dealer team who dress unusually: I imagine them shopping and deciding what to wear in a boutique.

I dreamt I was in a beer garden with friends. Two kids; two brothers come and sit down with a large lasagne in an earthenware dish. While the eldest is slicing it up we ask who made it. He is shy and answers reluctantly that his mother made it. I wake up crying thinking that the eldest brother represented me. Later that day I realised that it was the lasagne that represented me.

When my performances are documented often the photographer sneaks around to take some photographs from behind me. After returning home I take these rear view images into Photoshop and with the use of levels adjustment I bring to the foreground the faces of the audience who thought themselves hidden by the dark. I can see who was laughing and who was not. I have often been disappointed to find that people who I considered to be friends were not laughing and more than that some are even scowling. If they also have been temporarily afflicted redeye their countenance seems almost evil.

Walking back to the office to get changed the person who asked if you were nervous thirty minutes ago pops their head back around the door and says; "That was really great, here's your CD." Their finger is a temporary spindle.

In the methodist performance I photographed the audience when I returned home I adjusted the levels of the photograph to see who was laughing.

Drawing by Freeman White.

LE WELSH MAN'S 24 HOUR

24 HOUR SCULPTURE PROJECT

ENJOY GALLERY, WELLINGTON, NZ, 2009

In 2009 I made 24 paintings in 24 hours in Wellington, New Zealand. In a second hand *Subaru* covered with the funding bodies' logos I drove around the city on the wettest day of the year. I hardly said a word the whole day and I owe the completion of the project to some tough nut volunteers who battled against horrendous odds.

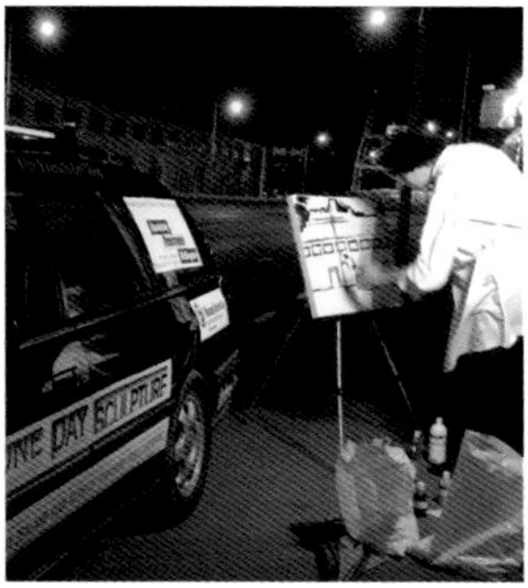

The paintings were auctioned and the proceeds were given to the New Zealand Prostitutes Collective. The money went towards the get together they are having in the picture. The red umbrella is a symbol of Sex Workers rights around the world. I could have done with one on the day of the project - an umbrella, any colour.

This performance took place in the Cavelerizza Royale in Turin. It's a theater which once was the Savoy royal family's stables.

This booklet was intended to bolster the fiction that there was a gaggle of artists in residence buzzing about Turin in a mini bus.

MINI BUS

ACCECARE L'ASCOLTO / AVEUGLER L'ÉCOUTE / BLINDING THE EARS

ARTISSIMA 16, PRODUCED BY NOMAS FOUNDATION, 2009

This performance is about a mini bus accident where all the artists in residence on board die apart from me.

LIGHTS ON

Screaming improvised.

Hello? Hello parla Inglese? Police...Emergency. Yes, hello there has been a terrible accident. Yes... I think everyone is dead. No I'm OK, I think...Yes... I was wearing a seat belt. I don't think I can walk very far.

OK, OK, wait let me see. We were travelling through the mountains we were travelling back to Turin, so I think we are on the road to...

No... no we are a group of artists... five artists... or artists in residence... it's the same thing.

OK, thank you. Please hurry. I can smell petrol.

Just before the accident we were all eating liquorice – someone had bought a big bag of it. Imagine dying with the taste of liquorice in your mouth. That's a real death sweet. In the post mortem the coroner will see black stains on four different sets of teeth. He will think it's strange. That evening he will go home to his pretty wife and while he makes his final approach into bed, his mouth fresh with toothpaste, he will tell his wife about four dead artists with black teeth and black tongues. She won't listen properly as she is reading a furniture magazine but during the night she will have a nightmare about being bitten on her huge buttocks by some people with black teeth and black tongues.

I read on the Internet you can overdose on liquorice – it can lower your testosterone and cause high blood pressure.

I've never really liked travelling with groups of artists, I think it makes me vulnerable. I feel like a gazelle that cannot quite catch up. The ability of a group to draw attention to itself is often greater than the sum of its parts. Walking as a group of five or six there is always one member of the group who will make you standout. Someone really small with thick spectacles

and a loud voice, who slows you down. Someone forgetful who leaves their coat or an asthma inhaler in a bar and makes you late.
Eating breakfast with artists and their puffy eyes, watching their fussy food habits you want to leap over the table and tear their ears off.
"Good morning. Do you have green tea?"
"I hope you don't mind, but I bring my own bread with me."

The allergies, the contact lenses, the special diets as well as the physical demands of walking around cities with people you would never select as friends. Sitting in the museum café eating a carrot cake watching a cute waitress brush the crumbs of a muffin into her apron you zone out as the group crowd around a map of the city and plan tomorrows itinerary breathing heavily.
I remember sharing a watermelon in Cologne with some students. Their stupid smiling faces munching. "This is very good melon." "Yes, this melon is very good."

Travelling in minibuses makes things worse. You are on display; an aquarium on wheels. It's a device for killing people, more efficiently in road crashes– it guarantees a strike.

I think I have one of Karen Baumgartner's teeth in the back of my head. When her head hit mine, her hair brushed against my face. I smelt her over-strong perfume for a split second. I imagine her apartment in New York smells the same as well, but also an over-strong smell of coffee.
She drinks her coffee like this.
Here I cupped my hands to mimic the supping from a biblical bowl, whilst camping with twats, style of drinking coffee.

The smell of coffee and hot computers makes me want to gag.
Coffee truly is ridiculous. How did a laxative that makes you talk too much become so popular? I dream of a drink that makes me speak less and shit less.
When I told Karen that I didn't care about fonts and typefaces. She said I was a 'Fucking Jackass'.

Before the accident about an hour ago Jyp de Kyp was telling me to chill out and to stop worrying about trivial things, now he's bleeding out of his shoes. The Chinese artist is dead – still listening to her iPod.
Karen Baumgartner looks like she is frozen laughing at her own joke.
The Peruvian guy is dead holding onto his mobile phone. He had been having trouble with poor reception all weekend. He was one half of an artists' duo and this was his first solo project. The other artist was texting him the whole time. What will he do now? Bloody artist duos. What do artist duos

do when one of them dies? The one good result is that the survivor gets to cash all the cheques for themselves.

As the bus rolled over I kept my limbs tucked in. In cars I feel like a baby giraffe being transported by a small under-funded zoo. Thankfully we were not travelling in a car without a roof. I know with my height that my head would be the first thing to go in a soft-top cabriolet type accident. Like a fleshy champagne cork popping off into the bushes.

I'm not bothered how I am dispatched but I don't want die in a 'head-off' situation.

Photographs of headless people are scary for everyone – I don't care who you are.

When the minibus was upside down, just for a second, I saw someone's sketch-book or diary fly past my face. In a movie, I would have glimpsed a drawing or a sketch. I actually saw nothing.

I often complain that I never get invited to go to interesting places. On the few occasions when I'm asked to work overseas I'm preoccupied with the thought that I am going to die.

I start worrying about it while I'm reading the first email inviting me overseas and by the time I get to the airport I am a nervous wreck. I try to calm myself down by smelling the different colognes in Duty Free. I douse myself in a scent that puts me in mind of a calm and relaxed man; maybe a European banker with a beautiful wife and fingernails that are too good to be true. When I arrive, I worry about the taxi and when I'm in the taxi I worry about paying for it. I arrive at the hotel and sit in my room for an hour or so; feeling anxious. Things get progressively worse during the week. There is a brief moment of clarity after a few drinks in a bar on the last night. But the truth is, that the whole trip is ruined by my fear and the curator who has invited me gets a bad impression and never gets in touch with me again, except for a few group e-mails.

Other artists seem so calm they eat salads washed in dirty water. They climb up tall ladders and take all kinds of crazy risks. I remember being teased for eating pizza instead of the local cuisine in Central America – after four days I still retained bowel integrity while the others became twitching shit fountains.

There are many times as an artist where I have thought I was about to die. With an entertaining German guy on some scaffolding. With a sound artist who had bad breath in a boat. With a curator who had a strange shaped head in Vilnius. But somehow I knew I would be OK.

So like Buddy Holly, Ritchey Valens and the Big Bopper, these fuckers will become legends and I get the survivor guilt and a thousand catalogues

that I'll never be able to use. If I decided to make work about this, their families would try and stop me.
"Who would want to see something like that?"
Their spirits are now walking into the afterlife with whole new careers to work on. Do they have to start all over again? Maybe a new CV or would it be a curriculum-ex-vitae? They may already have contacts there. Do they have galleries in the next life? Do they have Art Fairs there? Maybe Roy Orbison collects art. Maybe Howard Hughes runs a small project space in an old factory. It's probably a very different scene. Great openings! Everyone who was anyone will be there; wearing stupid spectacles and unusual expensive shoes.

I don't feel sad that they are dead. If I were to remove their spectacles or their shoes and looked at them I would maybe feel a bit sad. When I look at someone's shoes when they aren't wearing them I feel emotional. I think about their first steps, their school days, puberty, first kiss – I imagine their parents pride and then finally I can't stop myself from smelling the shoes and everything is ruined.
Line up shoes
The funny thing was that for an hour before the crash we weren't talking to each other because of a stupid argument; cruelty to animals, or something. But just before it happened everyone broke the silence with screams. The Chinese artist's quiet scream was one of the most beautiful sounds I have ever heard: like an expensive cat being punched very hard.
There are supposedly three stages of dying. Before, During and After. If you worry at the beginning about the stages, the second and third stage you experience is a kind of living death… or is that a kind of dying life?
The first two stages are horrible but I can understand them. The third I can't imagine. I can't imagine the first minutes after you die – as you power down.
At home in my house my socks are in my sock drawer.
The printer in my studio is on standby.
An aeroplane is flying high overhead and a car passes though the village.
In the other artists' apartments maybe there is a cat waiting with no idea of what's happening, in Peru or Brussels or maybe in New York.
I remember a beautiful black kitten that'd had the misfortune of living with a reckless French/Canadian bass player in a small bed-sit. The poor creature's faeces littered amongst the guitar pedals and pizza boxes like some kind of scat banquet.
None of these free spirits were wearing seatbelts. Only me.
I always wonder about those people who are afraid of flying that die in aeroplane crashes. As they plummet towards the ground, they must experi-

ence a kind of euphoria knowing that they were right all along. They see the Air Hostess screaming in her landing seat, as she is jolted violently in all directions.
A man I worked with told me about a small aeroplane crashing while his team played football in a park. The players and the referee all ran over to the crash-site. He said that sparks from the fire were burning through their nylon shorts. He said the whole experience was a buzz. When he told me the story his nostrils and eyes seemed bigger than normal.
Get iPod
You don't associate iPods with death as they have only been around for a few years but obviously there are people who have owned them and for various unrelated reasons have died. Leaving little bits of their earwax on the headphones. Earwax that will repulse some people but make other people break down and cry.
Musicians always use the phrase 'break down and cry' in lyrics – it's so lazy to use stock phrases.
Do composers and musicians think about those who leave this world listening to their music? It probably makes them feel good about themselves.

Jyp de Kyp chose all the music we listened to in the bus. "If I am the driver then I am also the DJ." he said. Visual artists are such music fascists they can barely play instruments but see themselves as experts. Jyp de Kyp was in a band he showed me a black and white photograph of them playing a gig. Young men with beards and serious faces. Coffee and beards and serious young men faces in a band fuck off serious young men. Serious young girlfriends.
Why would anyone have a wallet on a chain for god's sake?

It's funny that a guy who took himself so seriously has died with such a stupid look on his face. I would hate to die in an embarrassing position with my legs at strange angles or with a foolish smile on my face.
Rock climbers are often found after falling off mountains with their trousers torn to shreds only wearing their boots. I think that if you must die without trousers, that your shoes should be small and discrete – little deck shoes or slippers or espadrilles. Even worse than dying with no trousers is dying wearing big boots and a beard like a kinky goat.
YOU REALLY GOT ON MY NERVES DID YOU KNOW THAT? ALL OF YOU!
They were trying to get me to dance with them in a bar the other night. Forcing a tall man to dance in Turin – you fuckers.

The bus still smells of them inside. International body odour stinks like money and sugar. In small quantities not so stinky and sometimes even

PLEASANT BUT WHEN THE VOLUMES ARE INCREASED IT MAKES YOU WANT TO THROW UP. IMAGINE BOILING AN AIRLINE BLANKET TO MAKE TEA THEN DRINKING IT OUT OF A LARGE CUP.

I WORKED IN A LARGE LAUNDRY WHEN I WAS YOUNGER, WASHING AIRLINE BLANKETS. THEY WERE FULL OF HEADPHONES AND OCCASIONALLY VOMIT. ONE DAY, THERE WAS A SMALL EXPLOSION AND CORROSIVE MATERIAL SCATTERED ALL OVER THE FACTORY. WE ALL RAN OUT AND HAD THE REST OF THE DAY OFF. THE NEXT DAY, I NOTICED THAT THE STEREO THAT WE USED TO LISTEN HAD LOST ALL ITS MARKINGS THE CHEMICALS HAD BURNT THEM OFF. NO PAUSE, NO REWIND, NO FAST FORWARD, NO PLAY. ONLY A RED RECORD BUTTON.

WEEKS LATER, I BECAME FRIENDS WITH A NEW CO-WORKER. A RASTAFARIAN FROM DOMINICA. I USED TO CYCLE HOME WITH HIM. HE TOLD ME HE WAS A MUSICIAN IN HIS SPARE TIME AND WE SPOKE A LITTLE ABOUT REGGAE AS WE CYCLED SIDE BY SIDE. HE TOLD ME THAT HE RECORDED HIS MUSIC IN A SPARE ROOM AT HOME. I PERSUADED HIM TO BRING IN A CASSETTE OF HIS HOMEMADE REGGAE. ONE DAY, HE BROUGHT A TAPE INTO WORK AND I PUT IT IN THE MACHINE AND TURNED UP THE VOLUME. IT WAS TERRIBLE AND REPETITIVE AND ALL THE OTHER WORKERS LAUGHED AT HIM AND MIMICKED THE SIMPLE RHYTHM: 'DOO CHEE DOO CHEE DOO CHEE." HE LOWERED HIS HEAD AND TOOK OUT THE CASSETTE. HE HARDLY SAID A WORD AS WE CYCLED HOME THAT NIGHT.

I WILL HAVE TO MEET THE FAMILIES AND PRETEND THAT WE WERE ALL FRIENDS.

PEOPLE WILL SAY "AHA! YOU ARE THE SURVIVOR! THAT WAS A TERRIBLE BUSINESS – SO SAD, SO FUCKING SAD. SO MUCH TALENT. SO DO YOU MAKE YOUR OWN WORK?"

SINCE I WAS A CHILD I HAVE OFTEN HAD NIGHTMARES THAT I WAS IN THE BACK OF A SPEEDING CAR WITH NO DRIVER. THE CAR GOES AROUND TIGHT CORNERS AND DOWN STEEP HILLS BUT I NEVER SEEM TO CRASH.

STAGE DARK

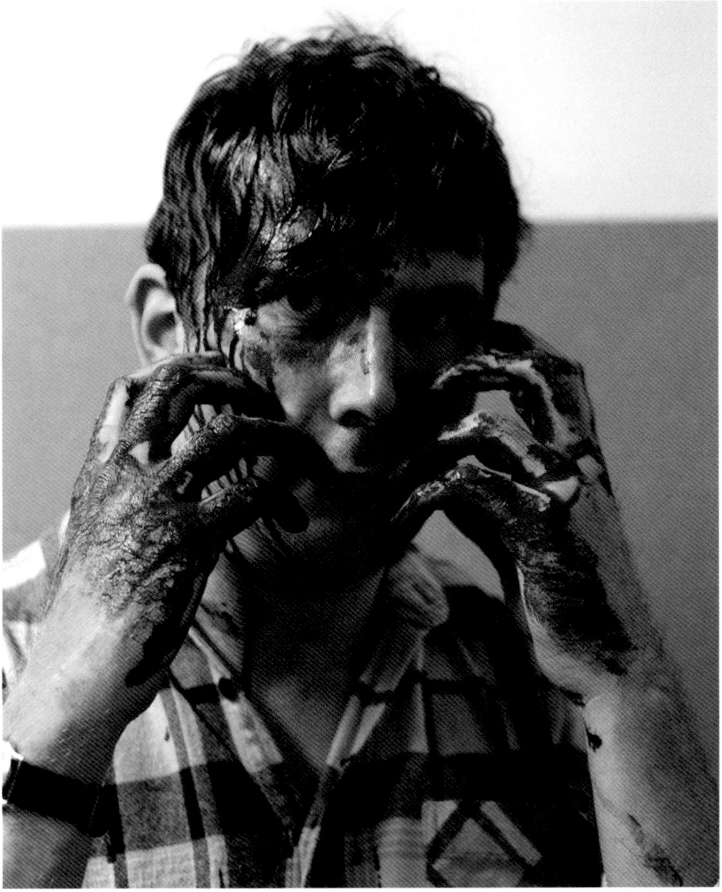

The stage blood was hard to wash off. Later, on the way home I walked past a military memorial service with some still inside my ear.

The chap playing the Chilean artist (left) fell asleep during the performance. It's lucky he didn't fart in his sleep or have a nightmare.

DUNDEED

DROMOS

GENERATOR PROJECTS, DUNDEE, 2010

I can't believe that I travelled all the way from North Wales to Dundee only to be hit by a taxi.
There are so many things I haven't done yet.

I haven't shown my work in America.
I don't think this will ever happen.

I haven't become friendly with a German Curator who texts me when he's pissed.

I haven't made an artist book with special fonts designed by a young designer.
I don't think this will ever happen.

I haven't made a large scale work which required grumpy technicians who arrive at work on fixed-wheel bikes.
I think this might be happening soon.

I haven't sold my work to a Russian Oligarch.
I don't think this will ever happen.

I haven't had a short passionate affair with a South American Trustafarian artist who makes work about the body.
This might be happening soon. Not really.

I haven't been on the cover of an art magazine.

When the police go through my things they will find a camera hidden in underpants, a sketchbook – a sketchbook! What a prick! They will find a grotty toiletries bag, that is skanky with toothpaste. A charger. A tripod. Why do I always bring a tripod? (*shout*)
That's my personal bag. Sometimes a few of the art things end up in that bag as well.
If I'm flying there is always the dilemma do I carry on the bag with art and check in my belongings or vice versa? If I lose the work then the show is off. But the other option is losing my things and being in Berlin or wherever with no clean clothes.
'I sink my boyfriend's is your size, you could maybe borrow his clothes.'

'Oh! Funny! Ha, your whole exhibition fits in a bag! The show in a bag!' A German guy said once looking into my eyes as he cracked his funny, he had a piece of couscous in his teeth.

I've crammed my work into cars and driven it all around the country sometimes barely being able to change gear because of lack of space. I've had bits of metal pushing up against the back of my neck on four-hour drives.

I've driven in vans with Dutch men through the night.

I've carried harps on trains.

I've been in cars with bald tyres and bald drivers.

I'm tired of the travelling.

In the beginning, it was fun getting drunk with artists from all over the country comparing notes. I used to imagine what they were like at schools. Sitting exams playing sports. The first kiss and a few years later their first art kiss; at college, with some hummus breath dreamer with bobbly tights.

Artists behave strangely; we all do it. In a barbecue with non-art people being weird in the kitchen trying to baffle people, being difficult and obtuse. But if it's something serious then I always behave like a normal citizen. A siege or a bank robbery. I've been in near death situations with artists and some of them continue with the artist act even in the face of death. Why act like an artist when a paramedic is putting a neck brace on you?

Artists often talk about how they would like to be buried in a casket of their own design or in a leather pouch. Fuck off! You're dead, get buried, dickhead!

There's usually something that distinguishes an artist from a normal person not that artists are ugly but they are definitely seconds or shop soiled – a slightly bigger eye, or small mouth, normal eyes and nose. Or small eyes normal nose and mouth. Or maybe just mad. As if they didn't come out of the mould properly. Like they are special. Some characters will cut themselves a silly fringe or a very harsh bob (make drawing) to accentuate their little flaw or quirk.

I've seen artists' bras hanging out of bags not normal bras but silly little look at me cutie pie bras.

I've see artists cry and pull horrible gaping moonies in bars.

I've seen artists twist their ankles in silly costumes.

I've seen artists in fights in squats. Respect our space! Respect our space!

Scottish and Irish artists are always bullying Welsh artists, making them feel small.

Artists that talk in child voices. Would you like a cup of tea? Signing off their e-mails like Munchkins. What's so funny? Why is everyone talking like kids? Things are bad, aren't they, surely?

Talking fluffy bunny jibber jabber as your tears drop onto your *MacBook*.

After the opening, you go out for a drink with some of the gallery staff and sometimes if you are unlucky their partners come as well. They are usually designers or web designers. They don't know you and they have probably been out for a drink with a whole load of different artists just like you. A Japanese one, a Belgian, maybe some Lithuanian character they had a long chat with about copyright laws.

There are the friends of the gallery, the slightly older people who help out. If you stare into their eyes there is a sadness, there that if you could be bothered to fathom, would break your heart and turn you on at the same time.

You get a little drunk with the gallery folk and for a few minutes at the end of the night as they point you towards your hotel, you think that you have made new friends.

Back at the hotel, lying on the bed watching a small TV in the top corner of the room, you drift off to sleep.

Waking up at 5 am with a travel hangover, no water, a tiny kettle not heavy enough to control it's own flex. And no friends.

After an opening, do people talk about you that evening in bed? Some fuck-head in pyjamas giving his twopennethworth.

Go back to the gallery tomorrow to get your tripod (*shout*)! Because you left it there. Compare hangovers and some meaningless shit chat with the dicks at the gallery. It smells of beer a little bit. This computer is so slow.

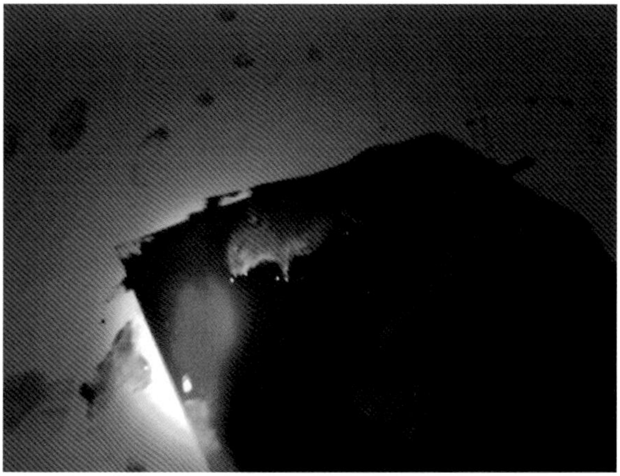

After the performance this mouse had been sneaking into the gallery and been eating the mint flavoured fake blood that I had left in the space. It killed him in the end.

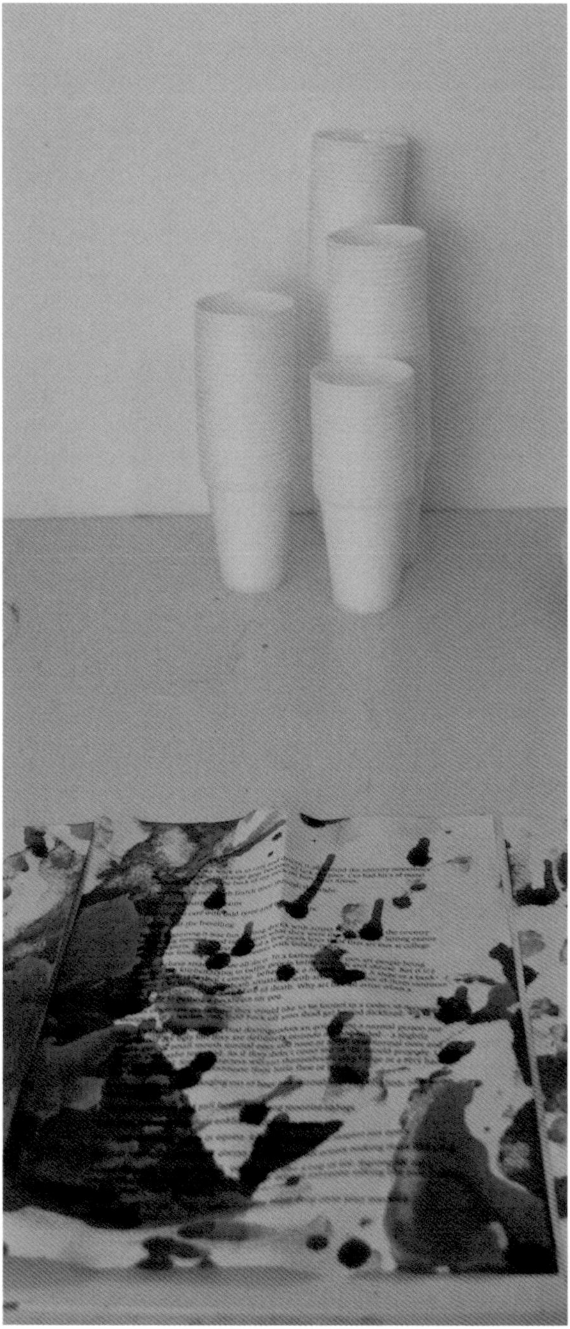

Fake blood keeps it's colour long
after the performance is over.

The art afterlife.
After you die, I hope there is an art afterlife. Maybe with Dead Artists Newsletter. Dead Gallerists with silly spectacles.
Dead Artists Led Spaces.
Dead Good Dead Artists led spaces.
Dead Art Fairs. I'm sure the artists that died young, rule the bloody roost with their ghost drugs and spirit shagging. Cold openings, with cute little dead gallery assistants.
Dead artist lead spaces. Afterlife Arts Trust. Nirvana Projects. Eternity Studios.

Dead Gallerists.

Dead Collectors.

Dead Critics.

Dead Sponsors.

Dead Networks for Dead Artists.

IN DREAMS

BLACK HOLE HUMS B FLAT

CERI HAND GALLERY, LONDON, 2010

Many people have shared their dreams with me over the years. At breakfast tables up and down the country munching on toast whilst their eyelids on a smaller, finer scale munch on the sleep crystals in their eyes. With coffee breath they recall the terrors and jollies of the night just past. Coffee breath stinks whoever you are. Attractive women are wrong to think that somehow this doesn't apply to them. I'm always surprised at how surprised people are that they have had a strange dream. As if it's an achievement, something to be proud of. I listen politely but after a moment or so my attention wanders and I lose interest like a windmill running out of wind. I have heard a tale of talking mugs of tea headmasters vaulting hay barns. Nightmares about small catering companies getting caught up in guerrilla warfare in far away countries. Fanciful dreams where pleasant situations are turned 360 degrees by the mention of a single word. I remember a pigeon-chested Swede babbling on about a dream where he grew feathers on his calves and wrists. Or the Canadian who dreamt of container ships passing slowly over his house. Other people's dreams are boring. Other people's performances about dreams bore me. My own dreams on the other hand never cease to amaze me.

In this dream, I'm very small sitting on a dressing table in a musty bedroom somewhere I don't know where. It seems like I'm there for weeks and the curtains are never opened. There's a Greater London funk to the room. Greater? Greater, shouldn't that be Outer? The woman who is sleeping in the bed wakes up every morning at 2.32am every morning. She sees messages in the digital display of her alarm clock. Messages about her past and future. A friend has suggested that she notes the messages down. She buys a little jotter pad with a shiny cover. The pen she uses has a picture of a bunny on it. Her sweaty grip is slowly wearing it off. I've been sitting among the makeup for ages and I realise that the make up is made out of poo. I gag and wake up. I'm in a workshop and I can hear people outside. I'm watching a tall man who is making bullets out of caramel. He's firing them at the end wall and they shatter. People rush in and carry me away in a sedan chair that isn't on fire but is smouldering. After being rushed through corridors for what seems like an age.

I wake up.

A goose with it's feet newly dipped in molten lead dashes across my chest. I wake up I'm in a conservatory eating a muffin. A woman in reactolites asks her husband.
"What y'er aving, Gary?"
"Bara Brith."

Bara Brith is a Welsh speckled bread. If you think my work is too colloquial you should have put the book down a while ago.

A man spoons out my eyes and puts them to one side. He places two wicks in the sockets and pours in wax. I can't see but I'm sure that he's using me as a living nite-lite.
I wake up.
A giant regrets eating a static caravan in Prestatyn as the aluminium tears his bottom to shreds as he passes his horrible meal. He has a cat of nine tails made with nine portable TVs, when it strikes me it feels like I'm being headbutted by a god.
I wake up.
I'm in another workshop making a coffin out of nougat – the handles keep falling off and I keep having to use bigger drill bits. The bigger the holes I make, the bigger the screws I need. I lick my finger and pick up the nougat dust and eat it.
I wake up.
I'm at an opening in a disused something. I put down my bottle and go looking for the toilet. I find a stall. Someone's obviously on antibiotics, I can smell it. As I begin to wee, I realise my shins have become enamel – vitreous shanks that chink when I knock on them with an ugly ring that has suddenly appeared on my finger. I roll down my sock and see a crest or a coat of arms as I try to make out the manufacturer's name.
I wake up.

I'm travelling by foot through a country. I happen upon a factory where they are compressing small aggressive men into logs to burn as fuel. When they burn them it smells like the seat covers of my old school bus – I wake up.
A graphic designer stroke musician who for some reason is in my dream – has a dream himself – of a scalpel cutting treble clefs into his scalp and smiles to himself. He wakes up.
I wake up.
A lasagne made with thick bleach and J-cloths in an enormous canteen – there is humming and faceless drones in gingham working in the background. I imagine their cold thighs gripping my head and squashing until I pass out.
I wake up.

A horrible boy with longish fingernails tells me. "I'm going to draw guitar strings on your face and play you." He fingerpicks my face until he draws blood.

I wake up.

I'm a wallpaper designer on a ferry during a storm. I have an idea about a wallpaper design which would consist of a repeat pattern of human veins. They are thin at the top and thicker and varicose at the bottom. As the boat starts to sink I run from one deck to another running away from the rising water I call a friend to tell him my idea so that it may go into production if I die. My friend says, "Just let me get a pen" and as he says that I begin to drown.

I wake up.

I enter a room and everyone who has ever taught me anything, including my driving instructor, are waving their hands at me, shouting "All at once" over and over again.

I'm sweeping up in a salon and no one is paying any attention to me. A fashion designer or something similar comes in and asks the hairdresser to make his hair look like sand dunes. The tondeuse fashions parched outcrops on the chaps tanned receedo. He does such a good job and it's so realistic that he starts to cry – they both start to cry.

I wake up.

A caterpillar dog is piling on the pressure he's so aggressive and I know him somehow. No I don't, do I?

I wake up.

A tug of war competition for mime artists – no rope, of course. After the competition is over they all sit down for a 'veggie curry'. I'm invited to join them.

But I wake up.

Vegetarians make their food less appealing by shortening the word to veggie.

A filthy changing room in a filthy swimming pool It's filth un-like waking hours filth it's dirtier, stinkier. It's a kind of meta-poo

I wake up.

I'm in a party with 6 inches of water on the floor there is carpet under there and some remote controls that I'm treading on as I walk – no one seems to care. I enter the kitchen and some mute students are drawing pictures of monsters onto the fake marble work top with crayons.

I wake up.

I'm walking through a street – is it Spain? Who knows. There is carnival music coming from somewhere. People rush from side streets, their clothes

decorated from top to bottom with lengths of carpet gripper rods. They try to welcome me with hugs but only succeed in scratching me. I scream for them to stop.
I wake up.

I'm running a stretch limousine company with an old school friend. We take some businessmen from a conference to a night club. In their briefcases they have large A4 blades that fit neatly into the cases. They try to cut my head off so I tilt my head back to try and stop them.
I wake up.

I'm installing a show in a gallery in Eastern Europe. At lunchtime a technician comes in with a stew and tells us to down tools. We tear off chunks of rustic bread and tuck in. I realise the other technicians are laughing. They tell me that the meat in the stew is actually technician meat. I try to throw up but can't. They laugh louder and louder. Their laughing finally morphs into a kind of hysterical singing.
I wake up.

Men called Gareth but who pronounce it *Garuth* in spatula shoes surveying a town. Their theodolites catch fire and rear up and stamp them to death. In a frenzy their waterproof coats with their noisy zips are torn to shreds.
I wake up.

You walk into a sandwich bar that has some Greek connections, there are pictures of football teams on the wall and some posters. While you decide on the filling for your baguette, you hear screaming from the back. Through a gap in the door you see two men giving an old woman dead legs. She has hiccoughs that trigger giggles which in turn trigger farts which in turn trigger even bigger giggles.
I wake up.

I find myself in a car boot sale in a swamp where all the cars are sinking. I buy a second hand video projector from an elderly couple who tell me that I remind them of their son. It must be too good to be true. Of course it fucking is.
I wake up.

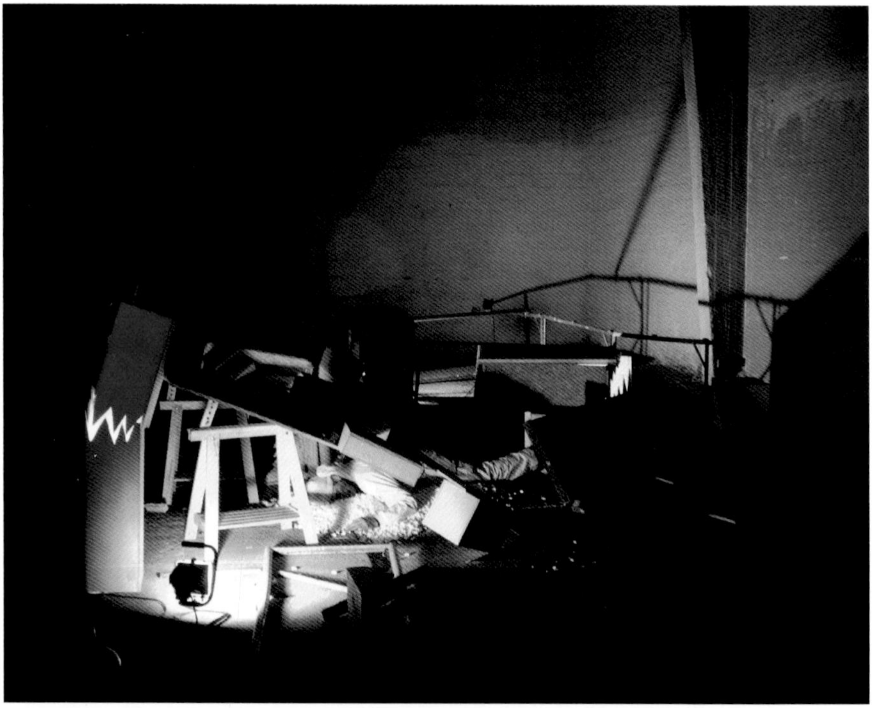

THE JYNX

1857, OSLO, NORWAY, 2010

Hello, Hello does anyone speak English? Can you believe it that I fell from the scaffolding and died, the night of the opening. I'd been so careful, it's ridiculous. I was really happy with how things were going as well – everything was under control. We were just starting to arrange the lights. I don't like heights, I never have. I think it's because I'm tall... there's more to go wrong. Higher centre of gravity means I'm like a big bottle of wine on a small table. I would never bunjee jump and, to be honest, I slightly look down on people who do. I didn't feel like I was flying, I felt like I was falling.

The catalogue has arrived. We were waiting for this all day and now it's here, I'm dead. The cover was supposed to be embossed, but it didn't work out. I wanted it to be a book, you know, just a simple book, with a normal font not something that looks like a manual to a pre-war washing machine designed by an idiot. I don't understand why art books have to be so boring. Youngish people revelling in dull cardboard and paper marathons. Font wranglers.

I wanted proper pictures not black and white halftone clever dick nonsense. I think people are ashamed to have normal photographs in books these days. Those that use halftone should be forced to sit down and reassess their life. In fact how about sitting them down with all those artists book dicks and throwing all their books on the fire while they are forced to read glossy magazines and badly designed bus timetables?

An artist's book burning. It would be one hell of a fire with all those fancy papers and smelly old fashioned inks. In a few thousand years archeologist will find all sorts of things that we use now. But when they come across a load of artist books what will they think? If they are baffling me now, what hope do they have?

"Publication." "My publication." "He makes an interesting publication." "She used to make publications." "It's an artist led space that make interesting publications." Give me a break.

I'm dead by the way. I just fell of the scaffolding. They told me to be careful and I thought I was but obviously not careful enough. I'm not very good with technical stuff. At college I was a joke, the macho artists all had drills.

I've made work in the past that makes joke about technicians, I was warned not to – that I was creating bad karma for myself and that it would come back to haunt me. It's like they are a secret guild similar to the Freemasons that will fuck you up if you mess with them. The Knights of De Walt, The Bucaneers of Festool, The Mercaneries of Metabo and Makita. In London, technicians have three letter names Dan, Tom, Nick, Dom, Gus. Their bicycles are carefully/carelessly customised. Brooding with their three-day beards and their trainers evenly worn. Jeans evenly worn. Watching your every move like sphinxes. They are good with their hands. Silent. Tobacco rolled up in their pocket. This is a guild of gits. When you use the wrong bit in your drill and make the dy,dy,dy noise, you can feel their irritation on the back of your neck. These one-a-day pooers. These experts. With the girlfriend who is as reliable as the drill, but with some bits missing. Cozy though. Cozy wozy though. Photographs of them on the shelves they made themselves in some fancy dress hell. With other technicians and their girlfriends and their three-day old beards. A thousand technicians will shake their heads when they hear them tell of the tale when the Welsh guy fell off the scaffold tower like some kind of deformed Pinocchio.

Well you know what technicians? How about 'Fuck you'? How about mister electricity putting on his blue tracksuit leaping out of the power socket and zapping the hell out of you? Dickhead. Or cutting one of your nipples off with a router?

This is a bloody nightmare. The last time I was in Norway I missed my flight home and it cost me £350, and the Hermasex who sold me the replacement ticket had zero sympathy. I spent three hours in Copenhagen watching weird guys with tattoos making smoothies. How much is it going to cost to send a coffin back? Everything is so expensive here. A coffin probably costs more than a car at home. Quite cool to have a Norwegian coffin though, a bit unusual. The artists that pretend to like me but actually hate me, will see the coffin and think, 'Hmmm, quite cool.' Artists often talk about how they would like to be buried in a casket of their own design or in a leather pouch. Fuck off, you're dead get buried, dickhead.

Will the gallery still be involved then? If the artist dies during the install when is it polite for the gallery to back off? Should the show still go on? What will the funding body say? Will it be mentioned in Artists Newsletter?

Who is going to empty my studio? It's a bit of a mess. Luckily, when I hit the floor I missed the intern by a few inches. I'm so glad I didn't end his voluntary stint with my head poleaxing him into the ground. I'm sure I could smell the washing powder of his clothes as I passed him. He didn't know what to do. I think he may have pissed himself. When you're falling to your death people's faces look so stupid. There's so much that can go wrong in an install. Fingers off. Electrocution, falling off a scaffolding, splashing

chemicals in eyes. It would be fairer to get all the guys on death row to work installing shows; it would probably kill them quicker.
This is quite hardcore what just happened. Curators like to pretend that they are hardcore. That they have no feelings. That they are like titanium emotioned immune-edons. But you put them in a dangerous situation maybe with a knife and a crazy and they will turn to shit in front of your eyes. I'd like to see a curator in an aeroplane that's taken hostage they would take their designer glasses off and hide them in the sick bag in case the kidnapers said "hey you with the stupid spectacles... come here..." "Who me...? I'm only the curator... please... no... don't hurt me..." Not like Demis Roussos.
Demis was once on a hijacked plane.

There's also the phenomenon of the hard-man artist. Take this and then add a bit of rudeness and you have a grade one stand-up – four on the floor arsehole. The kind of guy that makes you want to tear your spinal chord out of your back and strangle him with it. Put a rude curator and a rude artist eating together in an expensive restaurant and you have conversational Napalm. These people will cut you dead while you wonder how much their stupid eccentric shoes cost. Artists meeting each other for the first time are like dangerous dogs meeting at a car boot sale. They size each other up. How rude do they need to be to each other? Do they need to be rude to each other? Maybe just a little bit. Just like the bitters in a good drink. They don't know why but you need it. I'm worried that in the afterlife there will be an even more rude artists and curators. I remember as a young artist looking up at some Austrian arsehole in black clothes with a roller in his hand painting a high continental ceiling, flecks of emulsion on his sweater. He was literally looking down at me. In the paint shop the other day they had old paint tins – a few had a picture of a kind of muskateer character, d'Artaganan with a brush. This guy looks like a magician sex addict who also paints. As a ghost I'm hoping to go back and haunt some old foes. Some old artist led spaces that treated me badly. I'll loose their memory sticks behind radiators. Make weird half dog shit / half rubber smells by the photocopier and block the toilet. I am in a gallery office and you look at the box files and think – very organised. Yes, but for how long? One day these files will be taken off the shelves and not replaced. Someone will look through them and make a decision to throw the contents away, maybe one of my catalogues will be part of the contents? Maybe a gift from an artist that sat on the shelf for years. Some shitty chocolates from Latvia.
No one wants to see the inside of an ambulance. But being inside a foreign ambulance is worse. It is so cold here. I wrapped up but noticed some Oslovians who seemed to be preparing for pneumonia.

26/11/2010 — 08/01/2011
BEDWYR WILLIAMS
'THE JYNX'

I haven't seen a cat the whole time I've been in Oslo. I don't think they have them here.

I've noticed people wear strange headphones in town. They look like metal detector headphones from the seventies. I'm not sure if I like them. I ate Lutefisk, it wasn't so bad.

I saw an old woman on the bus this morning. She had fantastic teeth. Like blunt little china arrowheads. I thought about her routine: a coffee, some cake, see a friend, maybe have a nap.

I was just drawing a bird on the wall when I felt the scaffolding move. When I was lying there I could taste the kebab I had at lunchtime in my mouth. I'm feeling a bit tired now I think it's best that I stop.

Bye bye.

STEPPING RAZOR

CAMBRIDGE CONFLAB, WYSING ARTS, 2011

Guano is the excrement of cave dwelling insectivorous bats, seabirds, and seals. Guano manure is an effective fertilizer and gunpowder ingredient due to its high levels of phosphorus and nitrogen and also its lack of odour. Welsh farmers have adopted the word to describe all kinds of fertilizer. The word "guano" originates from the Quichua language of the Inca civilization. Welsh farmers mispronounce it and call it 'Giwana'.
They probably don't even know why they use the word or at least they have forgotten. When I was kid I was a non-farmer amongst farmers. They would speak about giwana but I never knew what they were talking about.
I didn't know what they were talking about most of the time. They had a kind of rural-polari-jibber-jabber that I couldn't make out. Their conventions and secret alliances.

I'd like to take you there now, if you'll allow me. Imagine yourself as a big mole in jeans and T-shirt and a pair of specially made pumps. Look down at the carpet. It's green like a field – a repeating meadow. Cut through it, it should be easy with your claws. Brush away the perishing underlay then there's screed (that's a stupid word) and then concrete and then earth, then clay, then earth. All that earth! Then going up the hill. Hills are bollocks. Burrowing for miles through the cold pressing earth. OK, stop now. You come out by a crossroads. You are steaming and you stink. You are out of breath and you put your mole hands on your velvety hips. It's immediately obvious to the other animals that you're an arty mole. Because when I asked you to imagine yourself as moles it's likely that you pictured yourself as alternative moles or at least moles with an interest in the arts. You remember this place; the bird song and the creaking trees. A horse box clatters past. The man in the Land Rover – the driver turns his head and looks at you – you have a pewter keel for a face, and two eyes like faded pressure gauges. You hear the engine change gear as he drives up the hill. You make a right and come across a farm in a dip. Giwana bags everywhere. The whitewashed buildings are filthy. There is a lame dog chewing on a chain.
The front garden, which is essentially a piece of field is fenced off with a cracked path spanning it. Either side tractor tyres painted and used as big planters. The paint flakes off after a while and then they are repainted.

A garden gnome out of his comfort zone. A washing line. A tricycle covered in shit. You look into the window on the window sill, you see a peacock feather in a vase, a pug telephone and a jotter with a bad biro drawing of a cowboy on it and a phone number. You back away and head east. You are offered a lift.

Stop imagining you are a mole.

You accept and open the door. There is a tobacco and private parts smell in the hot car – a Subaru. Tobacco first, and then privates as the passenger seat is tumbled forward. You glance under the seat; a Malteaser and an envelope to send your films in to be developed. You don't see those these days. You study the dusty interior, a fan of tax disks fading on the dash. A radio that looks like a scarecrow has been messing with it. There is a giwana bag on the floor to keep the carpet clean.

The son on the back seat – skin and bone – and when I say that, I mean skin and bone as in his face is a composite of both. His sweater a coarser weave than the rest of us kids. A big knit for a big nit. He spoke to girls and in a slow growling voice. This put most of them off but not all of them.

As he got older his proportions altered – like a marionette started by the head puppeteer and finished off by the inexperienced apprentice. I heard years later that he body-built and moved on down to the coast. Dispatched into the wrong parish and re-assigned. The paterfamilias, a kind of fore-shortened mimic Italian, his liquorice eyebrows, the punch line in the clumsy joke that was his life.

Mom tie-dyed in coffee. A noisette you wouldn't want in your mouth with her cod philosophy. In fact, the idea of these brutes drinking coffee is repulsive. They must have drunk gallons around that small table with the tacky oilcloth. Lower down the valley, another fucker welding without a mask. A fungal little git. An Albion lemur. Three brothers different sizes like different versions of the same tool – all blunt, one with a magazine of teeth. Friendly? Liked singing. Seemed to talk through his ears in stereo. The middle son a cretin's cretin, the eldest a sleepy basset hound minus the ears. Rock music dribbled into their lives. They misunderstood it and learnt the words as sounds all the while smelling of farmyard. You never really wash it off you just dilute it and push it around. Like salt deposits on suede shoes. Visits into to town to buy clothes yield some confusing outfits. Shoelaces pulled way too tight like corsets. They turn on each other from time to time but it's soon forgotten – and what I mean is they actually forget.

Opposite There are minty leisure people who move in. Their kids blonde and cheeky. English angels with whitish hair on their tanned napes, trampolining while the parents are indoors arguing over coffee. The new double-glazing means that they can be seen but not heard. In the lobby, the Labrador sleeps.

A grubbier setup downstream.

A filing cabinet in a field.

An arcing nylon pipe sticks out of the ground.

An electric fence.

A shot dog and the heartache that goes with it.

Lean to extension with a hyper thigh lady chancing a nude dash to the bathroom, the balls of her feet finding every creak on the landing.

For a man a woman's foot seems like a strange shape. Men's feet are funny feet shape like the ice cream whilst women's are closer to something from the animal kingdom.

The husband so busy in his 4wd collapses in on himself head rocking on ribs. Phone drops into his pelvis with his keys and wallet.

This is a vision too far. It troubles me a little.

In the village, at the bus stop, there is a couple that are not farmers villagers. She's coconut smelling, he's a sofa smoky. They are nice enough but they are obviously living in the wrong place.

I heard a tale of someone making toffee and letting it cool on the slate floor – but did not grease the floor first.

Ninety odd years ago, while the toffee was being made, what was happening here? You know? A cough, maybe? Someone yawning and locking up. Someone rolling a caramel around their clever teeth. That was here. I need to stop worrying about 'here'.

Back in the country, picture a big face pubic Pacman with mallow edges. Klaxon voiced and glassy eyed. A slackjaw, blonde girlfriend. There were nice 'uns, magical ones – elfin and natural. They were tucked away in dingles. The hedgerows leading to their houses seemed to herald the friendlier folk.

Above the tree line, harsher. Faces scalded their children's laughter blown back down their throats by the bloating wind as they try to play outdoors. A pub with a huge car park some fire beaters rotting in their stands. Dark characters from the city on occasion coming to do wrong up here. Imagine if your own camera tripod turned on you and was used on you like a weapon. One of the spikes touching one of your vertebrae for a second. A Land Rover pulls away.

Roll back to when the thumb was lost, maybe in the seventies – some clever people – maybe here – you know? Taking notes. Sun outside – girlfriend in a dress – unaware that someone's thumb is off hundreds of miles away.

A dead bird hung at each corner of the garden to scare other birds away.

The smell of food carries on the wind. Nothing fancy mince and onion. In a cottage some older folk. They are aggri smelling clothes wise, but eggy smelling breath wise. The man has little to do these days but look after his lawn. And that's where things end for you as you come up to surface. A spring loaded calliper folds you in two so fast that your stomach comes out of your mouth.

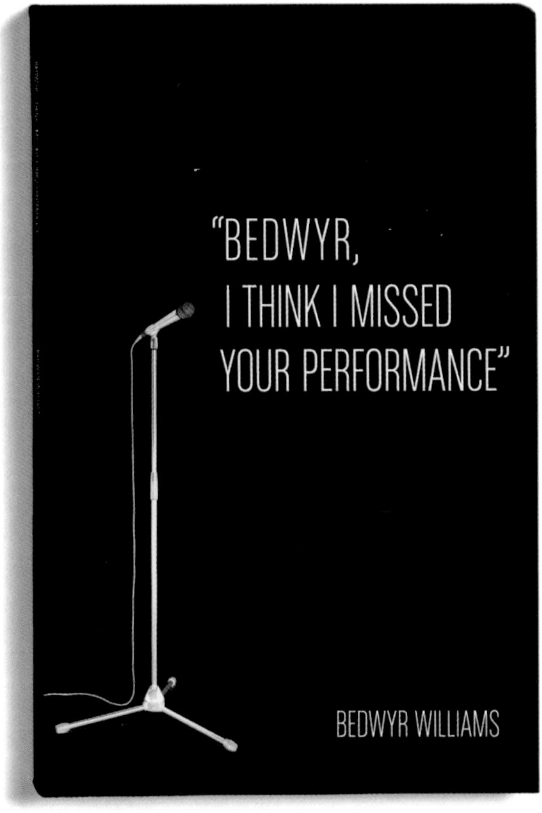
"BEDWYR,
I THINK I MISSED
YOUR PERFORMANCE"
BEDWYR WILLIAMS

URBANE HICK
A BOOK LAUNCH

This is the book which will be launched on the 15th of March at JVA at Jerwood Space.
Often my performances aren't finished right until the last minute. So this is a work in progress.

"Bedwyr, Hi, Bedwyr Hi, Bedwir, Hi, bedw-uh"
This is how posh people miss pronounce my name.

It's good to start with something familiar that turns into a mantra. That's where I turn up the weird to drown out the chattering from the back. The men with their pre-performance coughs.

When I take the footage home on a DVD or tape with my name misspelt on it in biro. I listen to the first five minutes and can't fail to be distracted by the throat clacking din of some moron, the John Holmes of the Adams apple world. A collar busting throat dong.
The name Adams Apple sounds like you can bite into it - what an excructiating crunch that would be.

A performance once it's done has a stink to it. A like dirty clothes. To use it again you need to turn it inside out. Until in the end you have a total stinker on your hands.

I remember one crimson haired teste-chops who obviously didn't enjoy my performance coming for a drink afterwards and scowling at me – Scottish style all night. I bought a round and dropped a Chupa Chups lollipop I found stuck to the bar into his drink.
That's made me think of having boiled sweet lollipops to replace your knee joints. A sticky arthritic hell
I don't know where the hell this is going. Don't be surprised if this bit doesn't make the cut.

English people go to extraordinary lengths to pronounce French and Italian words with a flourish. But revel in the mis-prononuciation of Welsh words. Even posh clever people do it to be a bit naughty. Performance art isn't an earner
Stop moaning.

I used to laugh at the 'I don't know what I want to do' possums at art school trying print making and then liking it. They've probably left London now, settled down have a space in a cute little studio making prints of unusual dogs.
Now I wish I was them
No I don't.

I'm not an ink feathers and poo performance artist. There's a kinship between some of these cacky ones that I can't seem to get an option on.

As a performance artist I aim for as little cleanup afterwards. That what spoils cooking for me. Cleaning the same hob every night - polishing your soul away to nothing. Hang on, this comment is better than the script.

Let's go back – in my last performance I asked people to imagine they were moles and come a crawling with me. This time I want you to picture yourself as birds. And like last time feel free to picture yourself as arty birds – maybe you have some feathers removed or clipped – others as straight birds. They dress normally to contrast with those who dress extravagantly.

I prefer the audience to think of themselves as moles.

Let's fly up to Charing Cross road. There's the tang of piss with the burning glove waft of crispy duck as a counterpoint. If we hover above one of the skylights in the building that occupies 107–109 Charing Cross Road. We'll see an acne whipped skinny malink. He's performing in front of a large VHS video camera.
The quality of those old things are actually really good – Fuck Off. He doesn't know what he's doing.

When I moved to London first I was like an Amish boy.

Let's fly East to some squat hell. I hate crusties. Check it out there is some live art happening, it's our tall friend again. This time dancing dressed as a chef. It's going well but he's upstaged by a drag queen. Is there anything more tedious and boring than a drag queen. Everyone loves a dame – well I don't. Drag queens are the live art equivalent of a ready meal. Ultimately unsatisfying

Let's fly over London – I like South London. All those futons in the nineties.

In the nineties It seemed like everyone in South London was eating grilled chicken and buying futons. I worked for one such guy. A big bummed Chino wearing fluffy haired sod. Futon, chicken, catch a film... Sod off.

We're leaving London now flying past those interesting underground stations on the outskirts

I love these pale outer tube stations. I'd like to go back in time and commute from there when they were built.

Good to get away from the filth and bickering.
London looks like a pretty unpleasant place on the news. In reality it is actually very unpleasant.

He's in Holland. Performing again. The Dutch misunderstand him and find him funny.
He misunderstands them and decides to move over there.

Stop imagining yourself as a bird.

Collecting live art sounds like those monsterous people who collect birds eggs.

You get a call. It's not a call, it's an email. Someone wants to collect your live art. To harvest it like rubber from a tree.

They want you to perform in their house.

You go by taxi. Like a stripper.

You enter the room. An assortment of middle aged curios. All pretty once save for one. Big bold jewellery to distract from wrinkles and sags. You ask to go to the toilet. No much wee comes out. It's the wee that you processed in the taxi. Not worth talking about.

Back in the room they are ready for you. They are all acting weird. Pretending to be disinterested. Who is going to be doing this peformance anyway?

I hate this cult of the intimate. Intimate gigs, intimate this intimate that. Sod off. Who wants to see a bloody band in their living room? Rocking out in front of your gas fire while you notice that there is a dusty sock under the TV.

One stands out. A lady in a business suit a cinched pinstripe corn dolly.

One man is dressed like an off duty soldier in the Napoleonic Wars, red stripe down his trousers. Stupid handlebar moustache. I wonder how far this dude's historic bent goes. Does he squat 'n strain over a potty after being out clubbing?

London!

Sunday suppliments keep me up to date with a niche faddy nonsense of London living. Going up/Going Down. These journalists should be barbecued until they squeak like the haloumi they love but I can't find in North Wales.

His girlfriend a harsh fringe frames a fondant face with countersunk eyes. She has a handbag in the shape of a realistic tortoise. He must be privy to all sorts. Watching his master's cooking, washing and romping.

Pursed lipped not judging until the zip running up the back of his neck is opened and his head drops limply.

Sitting on the sofa. A man with a livid red face. Boiling. A light coloured suit tends to his burns. His shoes a hybrid Persian slipper with the welt of a bloated brogue. He is cleaning under his thumbnail with an Oyster card.

Sitting on the arm of his chair a woman with an amulet around her neck. Pretty but the riding breeches were a mistake. Her asymmetrical bottom arousing and then baffling the others.

I'm interested in clothes and I'm always curious with shoes that border on panto. It's not just the art crowd. Reps and Bankers and lot of short men have been wearing long shoes for the last few years. Like leather spatulas.

More recently repulsive weathered army boots with zips on the side worn with trousers tucked in.

Horrible! Horrible!

All photography by Bedwyr Williams except

Artissima p4, p66, p73
Ian Brown p90
Collective Gallery p40
Pete Dibdin p18, p21, p28, p31
Generator Projects p74, p77, p78
Dewi Glyn Jones p27
Grizedale Arts p46, p48
Steffen Handlykken p86
Alex Hirst p80, p84
Juneau Projects p16
Hayward Gallery p53
Christina Oldfield p64
Mari Reijnders p8, p14
Nia Roberts p22
Anthony Rome p10, p11
Freeman White p64
Ffion Jon Williams p38
Llŷr Williams p8
Wysing Arts p92, p96

Urbane Hick was commissioned by Jerwood Visual Arts for Jerwood Encounters: SHOW, curated by Sarah Williams.

Mini Bus was curated by Cecilia Canziani and Ilaria Gianni, and produced by Nomas Foundation, Rome in the frame of Artissima 16.

JERWOODVISUAL ARTS

JERWOOD
ENCOUNTERS

Jerwood Encounters are a series of one-off exhibitions, part of Jerwood Visual Arts, a contemporary gallery programme of awards, exhibitions and events. A major initiative of the Jerwood Charitable Foundation.

JERWOODSPACE

Cyngor Celfyddydau Cymru
Arts Council of Wales

Thanks to

Mark Beasley, Pete Dibdin, Enjoy Public Art Gallery, Collective Gallery, de fabriek, 1857 - Oslo, Siv b Fjaerestad, Ryan Gander, Ilaria Gianni and Cecillia Canziani, Generator Projects, Grizedale Arts, The Paul Hamlyn Foundation, Louise Hayward, Hayward Gallery, Lucy Johnston, Dewi Glyn Jones, Iestyn Lloyd, Juneau Projects, Niru Ratnam, Nomas Foundation, Kevin Rei, Mari Reijnders, Ian Rowlands, W139, Emily Wardil, Ffion Williams, Iolo Williams, Llŷr Williams, Mary Williams, Melfyn Williams, Tim Williams, Wysing Arts.

'Bedwyr, I think I missed your performance' has been produced on the occasion of Bedwyr Williams' exhibition / performance at JVA at Jerwood Space

Designed and typeset by Sbellcheck

sbx.me

Printed by Out of Hand Ltd, Bristol
Editor: Bedwyr Williams
Copy editor: Alli Beddoes
ISBN 978-0-9568318-0-4
First edition date 2011